Here's Smiling at You

When life throws you a curve, hit it out of the ballpark.

Tony Ventrella

Publishing Partners

Library of Congress Control Number 2017955528

Edited by Frank MacDonald and Barbara Kindness
Design and Production Studio Pacific
studiopacific.com

ISBN 978-0-9714118-2-1
eBook ISBN 978-0-9714118-3-8

Printed in the United States of America

First Edition

Acknowledgements

To my wife, Mika, for all of her love, wisdom and wardrobe suggestions. To my children Lisa, Tim and Pete; my grandchildren Zo, Preston, Edie, Emmett, Angus, Zoey, Hadley; and my additional grandchildren, signed to late-season contracts for the sole purpose of making the playoffs, Madison, Karolina and Kaden.

Special recognition to my sister Mary Jane, brother-in-law Earl, brother Phil, and sister-in-law Fran. Thanks also for the support and love of my mother-in-law Masae, father-in-law Nobu, and our two cats Rocky and Pinky. You've all helped make my life complete and you've contributed to the length of this dedication.

Keep smiling !

Helping Mankind

By Robert F. Kennedy

We all struggle to transcend the cruelties and the follies of mankind. That struggle will not be won by standing aloof and pointing a finger; it will be won by action, by men and women who commit their every resource of mind and body to the education and improvement and help of their fellow man.

Here's Smilin'

O n one of my long hikes one rainy February afternoon, it dawned on me how strange it would be if we all lived forever. First of all, if you think the traffic is bad now on 405 through Bellevue, just think what a parking lot it would be if a bunch of 200-year-old people were driving 45 in the third lane. There's no doubt about it; there's a reason most people move on to the next world before their 110th birthday.

Speaking of that, if everyone dies doesn't that mean it can't be that bad a thing to do? I make it easy on myself by believing I'm going to a heaven where I'll see my parents and two sisters who passed before me, all my friends and people like Abe Lincoln and Joe DiMaggio. I won't need any money because everything is free in heaven, including Dunkin' Donuts and coffee. On second thought, cable might cost a few bucks a month. But other than that, I'm guessing I'll get along with no income and no savings. I remember someone once saying, "You can't take it with you," so I'm not going to count on it.

Now that I've settled that issue—at least inside my own head—I can go on with life here on earth. To do that effectively I believe one needs a sense of humor, a few good friends, a small number of mediocre friends, and an even smaller number of enemies so you have someone to talk about with your friends.

Here's Smiling at You is a collection of stories about the people I love, the people I like, and the people who couldn't care less if I like them or not.

I've tried to gather bits and pieces of useful information that may help the reader navigate this human experience; to at least enjoy it most of the time, if not every minute of every day.

Each chapter begins with a quote. I did that for people who don't feel like reading a whole chapter but can certainly tolerate a sentence with little quote marks on either side.

Since a picture is worth a thousand words I crammed as many photos into this book as I could to make it appear thicker than it really is. After all, one cannot be taken seriously writing a really thin book.

—•—

On one of my walking routes through the woods there's a big evergreen tree that greets me as I walk past. One day not long ago I laid my right hand on the side of the tree and said a little prayer. I've been doing it ever since.

I never pray for anything for myself except a better understanding of the world around me and clearer direction for my own thoughts and actions.

The world is a fast-moving place with a good portion of its population glued to a small hand-held device with no personality and no interest in one's well-being but loaded with information and entertainment—at least as long as the power holds out.

Our smartphones are fun and useful, but they will never replace the need for human connection and warmth.

I'm grateful for the technology we enjoy as long as it never replaces the feeling that comes from hearing a friendly voice, seeing a smile, feeling a hug.

I wrote this book to help promote more human interaction and more human kindness.

I've learned that being kind is more important than being right.

I've learned that just one person saying to me, "You've made my day," makes *my day*, too.

I've learned that I can always pray for someone when I don't have the strength to help in any other way.

I've learned that to ignore the facts does not change the facts.

I've learned that when you harbor bitterness, happiness will dock elsewhere.

I've learned that the easiest way for me to grow as a person is to surround myself with people who are smarter than I am.

I've learned that love, not time, heals all wounds.

And finally I've learned that everyone you meet deserves to be greeted with a smile.

———

Thanks for picking up *Here's Smiling at You.* I hope it makes you laugh a little, think a little, and say to yourself, "If this guy can write a book, so can I."

See, it's working already.

TV

CHAPTER ONE

Stick to Sports

*"Mothers all want their sons to grow up to be President, but they
don't want them to become politicians in the process."*

– John F. Kennedy

It was as close to a sports event as I can remember. My first exposure to politics on television was during my sophomore year of high school, watching the Democratic National Convention. As the evening wore on it became evident that a master of political maneuvering was at work and that his single-minded goal was to get his brother the Democratic nomination for president. Edward Kennedy, the relatively unknown third son of Joseph P. Kennedy, crisscrossed the convention floor gathering support for his older brother, John. Robert F. Kennedy had been a special prosecutor and had, in fact, worked for Senator Joseph McCarthy, the disgraced Communist hunter of the early 1950s.

Now working as his brother's campaign manager, Bobby was relentless in his efforts to gather enough delegate votes to give the Massachusetts senator the nomination on the first ballot. Bobby's brilliant mind and almost ruthless competitiveness, combined with younger brother Teddy's already adept political style, gave JFK enough votes to hold off Lyndon Johnson and win the nomination.

Early in the evening Robert's calculations showed that if Wyoming, the last state to vote, would be willing to shift its Johnson delegates to Kennedy, victory would be assured. Robert sent Teddy to lobby the head of the Wyoming delegation. Sure enough, when it came to Wyoming's vote, that state held the key to a JFK nomination. They moved the LBJ votes to Kennedy and the rest is history.

Even though I was only 16 years old and more interested in the New York Yankees winning another pennant, I was enamored by the workings of the political system from that night forward and to this day.

That explains why after giving it consideration for almost two decades, I finally decided to run for public office in 2016.

My first step was to call what is known in the political world as a "kitchen cabinet" meeting at my house in April of 2015. Attending the meeting were several friends from work who knew very little about the political process but excited about helping me. I also invited Sharon Mast, whom I'd known for 20 years. Sharon brought extensive government and campaign experience to the table.

At that first "kitchen cabinet" meeting were Seahawks co-workers Huy Nguyen, Jessica Hancock and Tiffany Green, and friends Stephanie Hemphill, Frank MacDonald, Tina Marie Mares, and Mazvita Maraire.

My plan was to run for Washington's Lieutenant Governor, a position being vacated by the retiring Brad Owen. The Lt. Governor is basically the referee of the State Senate and who only has a vote in the event of a deadlock. His or her job is to make sure the daily business of the State Senate is run efficiently and in the best interest of all the citizens of Washington.

The Lt. Governor also becomes Acting Governor when the actual Governor is out of the state. I was also attracted to the possibility of being able to champion certain programs for children, families and veterans across the state. No doubt about it, I had decided to run for Lt. Governor.

At the time of my decision I was working as digital media host for the Seattle Seahawks, a post I had held since 2006. My plan was to leave the job after the 2016 season and begin my campaign.

Shift in Strategy

In October of 2015, State Senator Cyrus Habib announced his candidacy for Lt. Governor and reportedly raised $300,000 at a single fundraiser in Bellevue. I must admit that put me off a little since I was told that $300,000 would be what it would take to win the election the following year. As it turned out, Habib would go on to raise nearly $800,000 and still only win the primary by two percentage points over Democratic rivals Karen Frasier and Steve Hobbs. In my heart, I knew politics was all about money, but I still didn't want to believe it.

About a month after that, my young grandson Zo suffered a stroke at his home in Colorado. He came very close to losing his life in the ambulance ride from his home in rural Summit County to Denver Children's Hospital. Thanks to the quick work and expert care at the hospital, as well as prayers from family and friends from around the country, Zo rallied and began to show signs of recovery in the first 48 hours. He has since recovered completely. It was determined that the stroke was caused by a blow to the head either while snowboarding, kick-boxing or general roughhousing with his friends. We are grateful for his recovery.

The shock of that setback sent me into a spiral of guilt. "How can I be thinking of a political career that'll take me away from my family for at least four years while my grandson is recovering from a stroke?" I wasn't raised in the Catholic church as many of my relatives were, but I still had a good handle on how to feel guilt. I announced to my friends that I would not be running for Lt. Governor.

Then I saw a feature on John Oliver's HBO program *Last Week Tonight,* about money in politics, particularly in Congressional politics. I followed that up by attending a Town Hall meeting with authors Wendell Potter and Nick Penniman who had just released *Nation on the Take.* It was a fascinating story of all the money poured into U.S. Congressional elections by special-interest groups across the country. The book also followed the money, finding that in many cases members of Congress voted heavily in favor of companies and groups who had given the most money to their campaigns.

While this may seem like a natural human tendency and is not illegal, it is a slap in the face of every hard-working voter who does not contribute to a political campaign.

Fired up by this new revelation, I decided to run for U.S. Representative in the 8th Congressional District, which covers a vast area from Issaquah south to Puyallup and east to Wenatchee. The district has been in Republican hands since its creation after the 1980 census.

I then took a trip to Washington, D.C. to meet with the Democratic Congressional Campaign Committee. Candidate recruiter Danny Kazin was very helpful and courteous leading me through a two-day process of meeting with research staff, fundraisers, political strategists, and a number of sitting members of Congress, including Steny Hoyer, Elizabeth Esty, and Cheri Bustos, Denny Heck and Adam Smith.

They were all up front and honest with me. "You'll need to raise $200,000 from friends and family before the DCCC will show interest in your race," said a staffer in D.C. Denny Heck was straightforward when he asked me point blank, "Are you sure you're okay asking for money?" I said yes. He was honest with me; I was not honest with him.

The fact is, I hate asking for money. Always have, probably always will. So I decided to rebel against conventional thinking and action and run a campaign without accepting funds from any special-interest groups or political action committees. That immediately ruled out the teacher's union, Native American tribal communities, firefighters, law enforcement, longshoremen and every other organization that might have donated to a congressional campaign.

It doesn't take an expert to know that my decision not to accept those funds planted a seed of doubt in the minds of Democrats across the state as to the level of my commitment to the race and eventually to the job itself. For all the public opinion about the dangers of big money influence on politicians one would think my plan would receive some level of acceptance.

It did receive attention from all the major media sources in Seattle, Tacoma and Wenatchee in Northwest Washington, but it was also met with a great deal of skepticism from radio talk shows and columnists who were convinced that I had no chance to win by accepting contributions only from individuals.

As it turned out, between filing for office in late May and the end of June I was able to raise around $20,000 from a group of about 175 people. Then I changed my mind.

Withdrawing

While running for Congress during the spring and summer months, I had also been doing a little acting in a play called *Plaza Suite* with the Woodinville Rep. This is not a good combination. On a Saturday in late June I drove to Tacoma to speak before the Pierce County Democrats. That group had endorsed me over the other two Democratic candidates, Santiago Ramos and Alita Skold. I assumed that this meeting was held to announce my sole endorsement, which would've helped my momentum in the final weeks prior to the primary. That assumption was wrong.

After hearing speakers in support of my two opponents, the Pierce County Democrats voted to endorse all three candidates. Needless to say that was a blow to my candidacy. A month earlier the King County Democrats voted to endorse Santiago Ramos while most of the local unions favored Alita Skold. Now I had a decision to make: Do I fight for the primary victory with lukewarm support from my own party or do I drop out and chalk it up to experience?

On Sunday evening as I drove home from the final performance of *Plaza Suite*, I said a prayer out loud as I often do.

"I'm a little lost here. I don't know what to do. Please guide me."

I never ask for specifics, just for guidance. Sometimes that comes in a form that doesn't immediately please us, but it always comes in some form and we need to be able to recognize it when it does. I pulled my car over into a grocery store parking lot and just sat there. All of a sudden it hit me. I decided I'd learned all I needed to know about a run for Congress and that it was not for me. I knew I would disappoint some of my supporters, but I also knew that my friends and family would understand. The next day I met with the media and dropped out of the race.

Ballot Rules

I felt immediate relief because of my decision, but only until I remembered that in Washington State once your name is on the ballot it's too late to remove it. I was on the primary ballot and would only be able to really exit the race officially if I finished third or lower in the August 2 election.

Having declared on local television and radio my desire to end the campaign I felt certain that voters would skip over my name and select one of the other two Democrats along with incumbent Dave Reichert. I was only partially correct.

On the evening of August 2, primary night, I was sitting on my couch watching a movie called *13 Days*, about the 1962 Cuban missile crisis. My phone rang and it was Santiago Ramos, one of my primary opponents. I assumed he was calling to tell me he'd finished second behind Reichert in the polling.

"Congratulations, Tony, you came in second behind Reichert."

"Are you serious?" I said. "You've gotta be kidding. I told people not to vote for me."

It was a strange moment. I had checked out of politics mentally and was, in fact, already looking for work in the media, writing this book, and overhauling my website. "*What do I do now?*" I thought to myself. I was stunned. Reichert had gotten an overwhelming 56 percent of the vote to my 17 percent, but in Washington the top two go on to the general election. I had a decision to make and honestly did not know what to do.

Media Calling

Within minutes after the vote came out, I got a call from KOMO television followed by KIRO-7 and KING-5. They all wanted my reaction to dropping out and finishing in the top two anyway. For the first time in my life I didn't know what to say. I asked them all to wait until the next day.

At 11 a.m. the next morning, with cameras set up in my backyard, I tried to answer some very good, direct questions from Essex Porter of KIRO-7 and others. "Will you run against Dave Reichert and give it your best shot?" I honestly didn't know if I could answer that question truthfully. I remember saying, "I'm honored to finish second in the primary, and I appreciate those who supported me. But I'm sticking to my stance on not accepting money from special interests." Then I made my biggest mistake of the campaign, although I don't regret it now. I was dead honest with my next response. I said something to the effect of, "I suggest that people who want to give to my campaign save their money and donate it to a charity. I'd appreciate their vote but not their money."

That statement was immediately read by the media and by my opponent as a retreat from the competition. "He doesn't really want the job," said Reichert in an interview later that day. "He can't make up his mind," said some of Reichert's staffers. One even wrote on Twitter, "Stick to Sports." When I read his post I immediately smiled and said to myself, "That guy might have a point." Some members of the media laughed at the notion that I would not accept money from special interests. "He's a nice guy but he can't win," was a direct quote from two mid-morning hosts on KIRO 97.3 FM. Here's a little secret: I knew they were right, but my name would still be on the ballot in the general election November 8.

Campaigning

In the nine weeks between the primary and the general election, I received plenty of volunteer help from my friend Sharon Mast, her husband Jim and their daughter Shanon. I also got some help from a group of students at Eastlake High School who were working on a mock election in their government class. By the way, I won that election with 60 percent of the vote a few days before the general election.

I filled out questionnaires, attended meetings, shook hands, waved signs in the rain, and on local television I offered a good argument for being elected. All through the experience I had high hopes of pulling off an upset, but deep down inside I knew what the results would be.

On election night, it didn't take long to confirm my personal prediction. I felt I'd be lucky to get 42 percent of the vote. The returns from Northeast Washington were dismal. I received only about 36 percent. I did a little better in Pierce County and much better in King, but overall I lost the election by 20 percentage points, 60-40.

Trump Wins

What would become a long and painful election night for Democrats across the country was over in a flash for my campaign. I phoned the Reichert campaign around 9 p.m. to offer my congratulations and left a voice mail. To his credit,

Dave Reichert called me back two days later to thank me for running a clean, positive campaign. Originally, I had thought Reichert might be a challenging two-year term working with Democratic President Hillary Clinton. Good thing I'm not a betting man.

As the evening wore on, it became clear that Donald Trump, who had spent two years insulting everyone who disagreed with him, would have four more years to do the same as our 45th president. I didn't vote for him. I don't like his smugness and thin skin and have frankly never thought much of his business practices either. But all of that didn't matter. He won. He would be president for the next four years. As a proud American who served his country in the US Army from 1964-1970, I can only hope for the best for all of us. I am not a fan of the "America First" nonsense. I believe all men and women are created by the same God and frankly He doesn't much care if his children are American or not. We are a fortunate country in so many ways and must never take that for granted. We are not special because we are Americans, but rather have an obligation to be special because we're blessed to be Americans.

As a free people who live in the most agriculturally fertile land on earth, we have an obligation to feed the world. As a free people blessed with an abundance of clean air and fresh, clean water, we have an obligation to see to it that both remain that way, regardless of pressures from business and even the White House to let up on sensible regulations.

Future in Politics

Lots of people have asked me if I'm going to run for Congress again. I'll get back to you on that. I'm confident there are men and women across the state qualified to make our U.S. Congress accountable to the people. Tomorrow's leaders must realize that the two-party system is flawed but can be fixed as soon as people realize that listening is more important than talking, and that the opponent's idea might actually be better than theirs.

A Reason to Smile

I'm smiling because I had a great experience in 2016 doing something that scared me. I didn't succeed at it, but I gave it a shot and that makes me smile.

CHAPTER TWO

Black-and-White Years

"Don't cry because it's over; smile because it happened."

– Dr. Seuss

I was born in the summer of 1944, 12 days after the Allied invasion of Normandy. My parents already had a boy and a girl: my brother Phil, born in 1933, and my sister Mary Jane, eight years later. In late summer of 1939 they had a baby girl named Joan. She lived only four months, passing in January of 1940. In 1945 my sister Bunny was born.

I like to describe my early life as one lived in black and white. That's probably because I remember our first television set, the first in our neighborhood in fact. It was a Philco inside a large wooden console with a tiny 15-inch screen.

In the late 1940s, anything on television was popular, but two or three shows stood out above the rest. One was the *Texaco Star Theater,* starring Milton Berle. *The Ed Sullivan Show* ran from 1948 to 1971 and helped launch the careers of hundreds of comedians, musical groups and individual stars. Ed Sullivan, the host, was a popular newspaper theater critic, not necessarily comfortable on camera but so well connected to the arts that he could

Me and sister Bunny

get anyone and everyone on his Sunday evening show, and almost everyone in America watched.

Sullivan produced the show himself and had a clever way of mixing in acrobats, the Russian ballet, opera singers, and young unknowns who would soon become major stars.

When a young rock-and-roll singer from Memphis named Elvis Presley came on the scene, Sullivan initially told his staff he would never book the hip-shaking, long-haired rocker on his show. He changed his tune, however, after Presley's appearance on the *Dorsey Brothers' Stage Show*, and later *The Milton Berle Show*. Once Sullivan saw those ratings, he decided he had to book Presley. The former truck driver from Tupelo, Mississippi, first appeared on the Sullivan show on September 9, 1956.

In later years, Sullivan helped launch the careers of The Beatles, Petula Clark, The Rollling Stones, comedians George Carlin, Rodney Dangerfield, Johnny Carson, and a little-known New Englander named Vaughn Meader, who did a spot-on impression of President John F. Kennedy.

Sports on TV

While one can watch sports events 24 hours a day on everything from cable TV to a smartphone, in the 1950s the choices were very few. I recall watching an occasional Yankees game on WPIX channel 11 out of New York maybe twice a month. Very few games were televised.

Boxing and wrestling made their way to the black-and-white screen weekly and enjoyed a large, loyal audience. I remember the Friday Night Fights, sponsored by Gillette, years before I needed to be concerned about shaving.

Wrestling stars like Haystacks Calhoun and Gorgeous George had more exposure on television than the President of the United States, who in my early childhood was Harry Truman, followed in 1953 by Dwight D. Eisenhower.

Radio was still king in the early days of television, but on certain nights at certain times anyone who owned a set was settled in front of it watching their favorite show.

It's funny but even today when I imagine the public figures I knew as a kid, I see them in black and white. Whether it's an emotional Walter Cronkite announcing the death of President John F. Kennedy on CBS November 22, 1963, Mickey Mantle crushing a pitch into the right-field seats at Yankee Stadium, or the disturbing images of Senator Joseph McCarthy and the Army–McCarthy hearings in 1954.

First Color TV set

When color television first came on the scene it was very expensive, but the few shows offered in color began promoting that service heavily. I clearly remember my sister Bunny seeing a promo for *The Howdy Doody Show* in "living color," then asking me if it would be in color on our then-black and white television set. I had to tell her no. Bunny passed away in 1956 at age 10 and never got to see color television. We didn't get our first set until the mid-1960s.

New School

In the summer of 1953, my family moved to Wilton, Connecticut, a small New England town that had been a farm community years earlier but was now part of the great push into the suburbs.

Wilton has a deep history dating back to 1877 when British troops raided the town of Danbury and retreated south through Ridgefield and Wilton, burning houses and destroying farmland.

I'm sure I knew a descendant of Wilton Militia man Seth Abbott, who was part of a small band of armed residents who helped defend Ridgefield against the British. My dad had an old hunting buddy named Archer Abbott who was born in Wilton in the late 1800s and whose family had a long history in the town.

I always found it fascinating that "Old Man" Abbott, as we used to call him, lived in the same house in which he was born and, in fact, died there as well. I remember looking through the attic of his old house and finding newspapers and magazines from the early 1900s. He was a fascinating character who was like a favorite uncle or grandpa to me.

Archer Abbott was a Yale graduate who told memorable stories to us while sitting in his rocking chair and smoking his pipe.

When Dad bought a small piece of land in Vermont and decided to build a cabin, Mr. Abbott traveled to the site on weekends, sat in his rocker and gave advice on everything from the framing of the building to insulation and roofing while Dad performed the actual labor. It was like having a consultant on duty who could also tell great stories in between giving advice.

When we moved to Wilton the population was under 10,000, and many of the small farms and apple orchards were still operating.

Dry Town

One unusual aspect of Wilton is that it was a "dry town" when we moved there and remained that way throughout my time there. We were not a drinking family and that's a good thing because one could not purchase liquor in Wilton anywhere until the law was changed in 1998, allowing restaurants to serve and sell alcohol. In 2009 the town council finally allowed all forms of alcohol to be

Wilton Little League 1955 (me 1st row middle)

sold in Wilton.

A very smart businessman named Elmer cornered the liquor market in Wilton for years with a store called Elmer's Town Line Liquor, just a few feet south of the Wilton border, in the city of Norwalk.

Special Zoning

My dad bought a two-acre lot in south Wilton for $3600 and built a small Cape Cod-style house for less than $20,000 in 1954. In those days if one wanted to live in Wilton there was no choice but to purchase two acres. The Town Council established a "two acre" zoning to help maintain the rural look of the community.

Living in a small house on a two-acre lot gave me plenty of opportunities for outdoor exploration without going anywhere. We had a large backyard that sloped off into a wooded area covering at least an acre. My dad had a garden on the south side of the house and kept chickens and a couple of turkeys in the backyard as his own parents had.

I was one of only three boys close to my age in the neighborhood and the houses were fairly far apart so we all did a lot of walking in those days. Eric Olsen lived next door and Dave Appelbaum lived on Bob White Lane, one street over from my house.

With only two friends living close by, I had to create solitary games for the times when we couldn't get together. I came up with two involving baseball and two more for football.

Our garage was built on a slight slope on the north side of the house, so the concrete foundation was exposed about three feet above ground in back of the house, giving me a perfect spot to spray paint a strike zone. I got my hands on a piece of wood the size of a pitcher's rubber, painted it white and placed it 60 feet 6 inches from the painted strike zone.

Since I was a big fan of Yankees play-by-play broadcaster Mel Allen, I not only spent hours a day tossing a tennis ball into or near the strike zone, but I also called every pitch out loud as if announcing a game.

Hitting Rocks

Besides "wall ball," as I named it, there was a game called "step ball," which was even more interesting since one never knew where the ball was headed after it hit the steps. The idea was to pitch and then play fielder. Since we didn't have high enough steps for "step ball," I played "wall ball," and frankly excelled at it. Let's face it, if my idea of a professional "wall ball" had taken off, I would've been famous. Franchise owners could save money by having only one player and save even more by having that player be the broadcaster, too.

Another game I came up with was "rock hitting." We had a gravel road on the side of our property where a couple of new homes were being built. I used an old wooden baseball bat to hit small rocks into the woods and again called the play-by-play of every hit.

I really liked my friends and enjoyed everything we did together, but I must admit that being alone was never a problem for me. I actually looked forward to it. It gave me a chance to be a major league ballplayer and broadcaster, all in one, at least in my imagination.

When we did play games together we also had to be creative. We became very good at fungo hitting, the art of hitting fly balls to an outfielder. That's a game that can be played with a minimum of two players which is often the way we did it.

Football involved an entirely different level of one's imagination. I used to love playing solo football after the leaves began dropping from the trees in our New England Octobers. I would always be the running back, and the idea was to run across our front lawn avoiding the leaves on the ground. As soon as I heard the crunch of a leaf I was tackled and would have to go back into the huddle. The imaginary huddle, that is.

When it snowed in the wintertime I'd start each play about five yards from the snow banks on the sides of our driveway and dive over them for an imaginary touchdown.

I wouldn't trade my childhood for all the really cool sports video games and online games in the world.

I'll let you in on a small secret. I still play "wall ball." Now I walk over to the local elementary school and pitch against the side of the building. I didn't spray-paint a strike zone since that wouldn't look good on Twitter, but I did borrow a piece of playground chalk someone left by the school and it worked just fine.

Wiffle Ball

In the early 1950s, a man in Shelton, Connecticut, trying to create a game for his sons, took a small plastic ball and cut some holes in it. He discovered that the holes allowed the ball to curve left, right, up or down. He then took a broomstick and had his kids play a simulated ballgame. As they played, the man experimented with more plastic balls, making different shaped holes. He finally came up with a ball that not only curved depending on the speed of the pitch but could be controlled by the pitcher following a few simple instructions. He named his new product Wiffle Ball.

When the game first came out the bats were actually wood and were sold separately from the balls. In the mid 1960s Wiffle Ball added the yellow plastic bats you see today.

Now, more than 60 years after the invention of the Wiffle Ball, the company continues to thrive and is still in Shelton, Conn.

Dave and Eric

My friends David and Eric played all the games I described above. With two-acre zoning everybody had a big yard, but our favorite place to play was a vacant lot up the hill from the Appelbaums' house on Bob White Lane. Somehow we found out that the owner's last name was Northrup so of course we named it "Northrup Field." I remember borrowing our dad's old-fashioned sickle, a primitive-looking tool that might be banned as a weapon today. We took turns hacking away at the hay and weeds and actually carved out a fairly nice-looking baseball field.

Each time I see Kevin Costner in *Field of Dreams* I think about David, Eric and me making a baseball field out of a pasture.

Every day we walked the half-mile from our houses with David's dog, Boychuck, a really happy, friendly Airdale, up the hill to the field to continue our work of creating our own little Field of Dreams, decades before the actual movie.

We even built a wooden backstop and painted the words "Northrup Field" on it. What's amazing is that no one ever told us to get off the land, and we never met the owner. When we finished we had a neighborhood picnic and all the families came to it.

I remember being amazed at my dad's ability to hit a softball. He was a hunter and fisherman with very little interest in organized sports, but at the first neighborhood picnic he belted a shot into deep left field and it rolled behind an old apple tree for a triple. Later he smiled at me and said, "You didn't think I could hit, did you?" I was so proud of my dad that day because I knew he only played in the game because of all the work we'd done to set up the field and organize the picnic.

Years later, I drove past the old field on Bob White. Not surprisingly, someone had built a massive house on the land. I was tempted to knock on their door and tell them the history of the property, but I didn't. Next time I'm in Wilton I'm going to do it. I wonder if the new owner can hit a softball like my dad.

Matchmakers

I remember one summer my cousins from Vermont came to visit. My favorite cousin was Janie, a year younger than I and filled with an adventurous spirit. Her older sister Jean Anne and my friend David were the same age. They seemed to get along pretty well that summer.

Janie recalled in a recent conversation how David, who played piano, entertained Jean with a classical piece he'd learned. She was impressed. We rolled our eyes.

Wilton Grows

In 1977, I left Connecticut for a television job in Fort Wayne, Indiana. A few years prior to that my parents sold their home in Wilton and moved north to Danbury. In the mid 1980s, someone bought our old house, demolished it and built a 5,700 square-foot house. I'm not certain, but I will guess they didn't build it for less than $20,000.

Today, Wilton is home to several successful companies and, in fact, has an average family income of $310,000 a year. Many of the residents still commute to New York City on the train from Wilton Center. It's about a 55-minute ride to Manhattan.

Notable Names

When I lived in Wilton in the 50s and early 60s I knew we had a few famous people in our midst. My friend Tenner Sterling's dad was a skilled furniture maker and among his clients was actress Bette Davis. I was also thrilled to find out that Raymond Massey, who played President Lincoln in *Lincoln of Illinois*, also lived in Wilton.

Joyful Sundays

My mom took us to the Christian Science Church in Wilton Center every Sunday. In our church, students could attend Sunday school classes until the age of 20. After that they'd join the adults in the main church upstairs.

Me, Mom & Bunny
in Vermont

I enjoyed the Sunday service, but I'd be less than honest if I didn't admit that the experience got even better when I found out we had a famous actress named Joy Harmon in our midst.

Keep in mind that in the late 1950s into the early 60s Marilyn Monroe and Jayne Mansfield were battling for the hearts and imaginations of men all over the world, including this young man.

Joy Harmon was much less famous than Marilyn or Jayne, but the well-endowed blonde from my hometown was no less gorgeous.

She appeared in several television shows during the 60s, including *Gomer Pyle, USMC, My Three Sons, The Beverly Hillbillies,* and *Batman.* There is no doubt, however, that Joy Harmon is best known for the carwash scene in the movie *Cool Hand Luke,* starring Paul Newman.

One Sunday I wandered into church ready to hear the weekly lesson and absorb some positive thoughts to carry with me through the coming week.

Either God was testing me or teasing me because Miss Harmon sat down in the same pew, a few feet to my left, just before the service began. I'm sure I heard the lesson that day from the two readers, but I'm also sure not much of it sank in. My brain and hormones were too busy digesting the brush with greatness I was enjoying. After church I went home and washed my car.

Jenny O'Neill

Of all the famous people living in Wilton then and now, my favorite was actress Jennifer O'Neill, who appeared in a number of motion pictures, most notably playing a war bride named Dorothy in *Summer of 42,* which was showing in theaters in 1972.

A decade earlier, as a high school junior, I drove to school by the same route every day, and one day in the cafeteria an eighth grader named Jenny O'Neill asked me if I would mind picking her up at her bus stop so she wouldn't have to take the bus to school. I said, "Sure, ask your parents first, and if they say it's okay you can ride with me to school." They gave her permission and for the next two school years I drove Jenny to school.

Years later, when *Summer of 42* was in release, I called her at her home in New Rochelle, New York, and asked if I could bring some local teens to meet her. I was shocked when she said, "Sure, Tony, and by the way, I remember that cool 1961 Corvair you had and all those rides to school." Chevrolet made the Corvair model from 1960-69. It had a rear engine whose fan belts broke all the time, but not once during my trips to school with Jenny O'Neill. I explained that I was Director of the Wilton Youth Project Drama program and some of the teens wanted to meet a professional actor.

A few days later we piled into two cars and drove from Wilton to New Rochelle to see Jennifer. It had been ten years since my graduation from Wilton High since I'd seen her. She greeted me with a hug, which impressed the heck out of the students, and then we all sat in her living room and talked about the movie and her career.

I was too embarrassed to ask for her autograph, and besides I already had one anyway. On the last day of school in my senior year she signed my yearbook. It says, "Love, Jenny," and I can prove it.

A Reason to Smile

Summer of 42 remains one of my favorite movies today. I make it a point to watch it once a year, in the summer.

CHAPTER THREE

The Big Trade

*"We didn't realize we were making memories,
we just knew we were having fun."*

– Winnie the Pooh

The Viet Nam war cost 58,220 American military lives, including four from my hometown of Wilton, Conn. One of the young men was Johnny Corr.

I knew Johnny in high school. I watched him lead the football team under Coach Nick Zeoli to an undefeated season and Class C state title in 1961. I saw him lead the basketball team to a Western Connecticut Conference championship and the track team to an undefeated season.

After graduation, Johnny went to the University of Bridgeport and led their football team to three successful seasons.

One summer evening in 1966, I was running on the high school track and ran into Johnny. I remember his exact words that day. "Wish me luck. I just joined the Gyrenes," a rarely used term meaning Marines. I shook his hand and wished him luck.

First Lt. John Corr was wounded three times in battle in Viet Nam. The third time—in December of 1967—he was killed.

I knew Johnny in high school, but we met long before that, in fourth grade. We played on Miss Hoag's fifth grade softball team together and during the summer played recreation basketball on the same team.

In the summer of 1955, Eisenhower was president, Elvis Presley had just recorded "Hound Dog" and "Blue Suede Shoes," and the Brooklyn Dodgers finally won a World Series, beating the Yankees in seven games.

It was the last day of fifth grade at Center School. Miss Hoag had finished teaching us the capitals of every state, how to draw a good map, proper grammar and penmanship and, most of all for me, how to hit a softball to the opposite field for a base hit.

Johnny and I were both baseball fans and we both collected baseball cards in huge numbers. All during the school year we talked about which cards we had and which ones we wanted. At one point we determined that I had two Mickey Mantles and needed a Willie Mays, and he had two Willies and needed a Mickey. We planned the big player trade for the last day of school at my house.

My cards were sorted by year, league and team. Keep in mind that many of the cards we took for granted in those days, like Mantle, Mays, Duke Snider and Ted Williams, are worth in some cases thousands of dollars today in mint condition.

We bought them for ten cents a pack at the local candy store and that included the slab of rock hard bubble gum that could've been used as a weapon, if needed. It had an amazing burst of flavor that lasted a very short time. In fact, once for the fun of it, I timed it. My Topps bubble gum lost its flavor in just under 21 seconds on a good day.

In those days, baseball cards were only available at some stores. Grocery stores didn't carry them, and there were no big box stores so we had to rely on Stiver's Drug Store in Wilton Center or Herman's Smoke Shop in Norwalk. Luckily for me, my friend Dave Appelbaum's dad was a doctor who had an office not far from Herman's, so a couple times a month we'd hitch a ride with Dr. Appelbaum to Herman's for our cards. Even though I never smoked, I still have sweet memories of Herman's Smoke Shop and the aroma of pipe tobacco hanging in the air. Everything in Herman's smelled like tobacco, including the packs of baseball cards. Now that I think about it, even Herman smelled like pipe tobacco.

Johnny took a different bus home than I did, so his mom had to drive him over to my house around 4 o'clock. By the time he reached my house I had three shoe boxes of cards set up on the front porch. Even though it was Mickey

Mantle he wanted he still wanted to see who else I had. It was part of being a little kid in the 1950s.

At exactly 4 p.m. Johnny's mom pulled into the driveway with their 1953 Ford station wagon and Johnny hopped out. "Pick you up at 6," his mom said. Johnny nodded and she drove off.

We showed off our cards for a while, and then it was time for the big deal. As I think back now, it seems like we handed those cards over in slow motion. I handed Mantle to Johnny; he handed Mays to me. Now our collections were complete.

We put the cards away and played Wiffle Ball until Johnny's mom came to pick him up. It's funny to think about now, but in all the years I knew Johnny that was the only time he came to my house. That made the "Big Deal" even bigger in my memory.

After Johnny died, Wilton High School created an annual award in his name. The Lt. John G. Corr Memorial Award is presented at the end of each school year to a deserving Wilton High School senior who shows courage and leadership on and off the football field.

The inscription on the award, dated December 28, 1967, is as follows: In memoriam to a young man, Wilton High School graduate and Wilton native who served his country and paid the supreme sacrifice.

Rest of the Story

One of Johnny's best friends was classmate Bill Hack. Bill played fullback behind Johnny in high school and for three years in college. Five years ago, at a class reunion he told this story.

"I was stationed at the Patuxent River Naval Station in Maryland in the summer of 1969. The Catholic chaplain was a gregarious fellow easy to engage in conversation. During one of our chats I asked him where he'd been stationed previously. He mentioned he was a Navy chaplain for a Marine unit in Viet Nam. He asked me about my background, and I told him I grew up in Wilton, Conn. His eyes widened and almost interrupting me he said, 'I've gotta tell you, Bill, the bravest Marine I ever met was from Wilton. He was always at the point and led his men with extraordinary courage. He was fearless. His name was Johnny Corr.'"

A Reason to Smile

I visited the Viet Nam War Memorial the last time I was in Washington, D.C. It does make me sad, but as soon as I touch his name on the wall and say a short prayer I'm smiling again, grateful to have known Johnny for a few short years.

CHAPTER FOUR

Goodbye Anthony

"No matter how many times you fall in love after your first love, they will always be in your heart."

My father's name was Anthony, so when I was born the second son in the family, my parents named me Anthony Jr. For all of my early childhood, everyone called me Anthony, except on occasions when my mother for some reason called me Tommy. She said she didn't want to call out the name Anthony when my dad was within earshot since that might be confusing, so on some days I was Tommy, but usually Anthony.

That ended in 1960, my junior year in high school. I don't know why it ended. I'm not sure who started it, but I know someone started calling me Tony, and it stuck from that day forward. Actually, it didn't stick at home, where my parents still called me Anthony and occasionally Tommy. Years later when I got into the broadcasting business, everyone called me Tony.

The year 1960 was a memorable one for me on so many levels. I got my driver's license in June of that year and immediately took the 1957 Plymouth my sister Mary Jane and I had bought together and drove it to Wilton Center for no particular reason. Then I drove back down Belden Hill Road to my house, picked up mom's car and drove that to the grocery store and back.

By then my dad was home with his brand-new 1960 Dodge with really cool reverse tail fins and the first automatic windows I'd ever seen on a car. With his permission, I drove the new Dodge back to the grocery store for something I'd forgotten on purpose on the previous trip. I had successfully driven every car in the family the first day I had my license.

The first year of the decade was filled with so many other highlights I probably can't include them all in a book, let alone a single chapter, but I'll cover the big ones.

As you know by now, I was and always will be a New York Yankees fan. I have my Uncle Fred Schilling to thank for that. He was Vice President of Turner Construction Company in New York City and had company box seats at Yankee Stadium. The first time I saw Mickey Mantle was in 1956 from a box seat next to the Yankees dugout.

Now, four years later, the Yankees were again dominating the American League in search of another pennant and World Series title.

In the World Series that year they faced the Pittsburgh Pirates in what was, according to some baseball historians, the greatest World Series ever played. Certainly game seven on October 13, 1960 was one of the greatest single games ever played.

The Pirates had won the National League pennant with a record of 95-59. They had terrific pitching led by Elroy Face and Vernon Law. They had one of the best players in the history of the game in outfielder Roberto Clemente. Their second baseman was a guy named Bill Mazeroski, certainly a good ballplayer before the '60 Series and one whose name would live in immortality as a result of it.

The series opened on October 5 at Forbes Field in Pittsburgh with the Yankees a huge favorite. The Pirates won the game, 6-4. The next day the Yankees, behind Mantle's two homers, romped, 16-3.

At Yankee Stadium two days later Whitey Ford shutout the Pirates, 10-0, second baseman Bobby Richardson had a record six RBI, and it looked like the Yankees would make short work of the series. It was not to be.

The Pirates behind Vernon Law managed a 3-2 win in game four to lock the series at two games apiece. Lefty Harvey Haddix made it two in a row with a 5-2 victory in game five. They would head back to Pittsburgh with the Pirates leading the series three games to two.

In game six Whitey Ford dominated the Pirates 12-0 to keep his World Series scoreless innings streak intact and tie the series at 3-3.

On October 13, beautiful mid-autumn weather greeted the sellout crowd at Forbes Field as Haddix faced off with Yankees right-hander Ralph Terry.

I remember watching the game on live black-and-white television in my living room. All the games were in the afternoon in those days, so I had rushed home from school to record the audio on my reel-to-reel recorder, a tape I still have today.

The game went back and forth with the teams exchanging the lead a couple of times. Manager Ralph Houk summoned right hander Ralph Terry to pitch the bottom of the 10th inning. He was the fifth Yankee pitcher that afternoon. The Pirates also used five.

With the bases empty, Mazeroski stepped to the plate and hit a Terry fastball just over the left-field fence for the game- and series-winning home run. I will never erase the image of left fielder Yogi Berra watching that ball float over the fence and into baseball history.

For this young Yankee fan, that still remains the most disappointing day of my life. I know it sounds crazy, but I may have never gotten over that moment, even though the Yankees have won nine World Series since that October day in 1960.

JFK Elected

A few weeks later, a young senator from Massachusetts named John F. Kennedy won the closest presidential election in history. That made me feel a little better.

I've described three events in 1960 that have definitely left an imprint on my memory, but there is a fourth occurrence that happened in the late summer of that year that touched my soul as nothing had before and nothing has since.

Doris

On one of our frequent family trips to see relatives in Rutland, Vermont, I met a girl. Not just any girl but one that would remain etched in my memory for the rest of my life.

It was a chilly weekday evening in early September. I was visiting my favorite cousin Janie Garofano and her large family on Union Street in Rutland. She was just beginning her sophomore year at Mt. St. Joseph High School. Jane was a gregarious teen with lots of friends and a bit of a rebellious nature. Her two closest friends were Betty and Doris.

Since the three friends lived fairly close together in Rutland, they often gathered at one of their houses. Betty's house was in the middle of the three so they most often met there. Yet on this particular night we all gathered at my cousin Jane's, at 54 Union Street. That's where I met Doris on a summer evening in early September of 1960.

Doris was about 5'5" with short blonde hair and hazel eyes. I couldn't take my eyes off her, though I don't think it was obvious. I remember saying some silly things to make her laugh and when she did I was hooked. Somehow, over the next hour or so, I got up the nerve to ask her to go to the Rutland Fair the next night.

The Vermont State Fair on South Main Street in Rutland, Vermont, has been around since 1846. It is famous throughout New England as an agricultural fair with all the rides, events and entertainment one might expect at a major late summer event.

In fact, it was at the Rutland Fair that I first saw Vaughn Meader, a comedian who did a spot-on impression of John F. Kennedy and later released a 33 1/3 album called *First Family*, still one of the funniest recordings I've ever heard.

The Rutland Fair took place in early September every year until 2016 when it was moved back to mid-August.

Doris didn't hesitate to answer "yes" to my request and we quickly made plans to meet the next night at the fairgrounds.

I was staying in Danby, about 35 miles south of Rutland, with my family. My cousin Robert's mom and dad had a cabin next to ours, and I remember borrowing his red sweater to wear on my date. The weather that September evening in Vermont was quite chilly.

My cousin Robert dropped me off at the front entrance to the fair, and there was my new friend Doris, looking even cuter than I remembered from the evening before.

Life is a series of small events. Some are forgotten almost immediately. Some remain with us forever, going dormant for a time until the memory is triggered by one of our senses.

In the decades since my first and only date with Doris, I've been to various state and county fairs all over the country, and every time I go one of my senses reminds me of that September night in Vermont.

Every state fair is a little unique and yet so similar to the others. In the 1960s Rutland still had a large Italian-American population, so you would immediately smell the aroma of sausage and pepper grinders, pizza by the slice, and a deep-fried dough, sweetened with sugar, referred to by some as "Zeppoli." Every fair I've been to since then has offered a similar treat with a different name. I've heard it referred to as a funnel cake in New York and an Elephant Ear at the Washington State Fair in Puyallup.

My point is that those food aromas remain with us for life and trigger memories of years gone by like nothing else can.

I suppose you could say the same about the livestock barns as well, though it's an aroma one tolerates for a few minutes but doesn't necessarily look forward to. "Oh, look at the baby cows. How cute. Now, let's get out of here."

Doris and I walked through every inch of the Rutland Fair on that September night, past the game booths with men urging me to "win a prize for the lady" by shooting a rifle with bad sights at moving targets, all for the chance to win a prize worth a fraction of what it cost to play the game.

We passed the side shows near the back of the fair where characters—dressed in jackets, frilly shirts with bow ties and shiny shoes—waved us towards the entrance. "You won't believe it until you see it, the two-headed boy! Half-boy, half-beast! Step right up!" Even if I did want to see the two-headed boy or the tallest man in the world or the fire eater, I would've never admitted it to Doris.

As we walked around the fair I was in full comedian mode, though I'm sure a good portion of my little show was meant to cover up for how fast I was falling for this quiet, shy, angelic 15-year-old girl from Rutland, Vermont.

I've never been a fan of carnival rides, especially the Ferris wheel, so when we got to that part of the fair I had a decision to make. Do I tell her the truth or fake it and go on the ride anyway? I decided to tell the truth. If she'd insisted on going on a ride, I would've done it in a second but she didn't. She just brushed it off like it wasn't important to her either. How could I have found such a perfect girl? She laughed at my jokes and didn't like rides either, or at least said she didn't so I wouldn't feel bad.

Toward the end of the evening it got really cold and it was time for her to get home. I remember walking her home along the quiet streets of Rutland and at one point, about halfway home, I reached for her hand. For me that was a bold move. Jokes were not a problem, but holding a girl's hand on the first date in 1960, that was not a given.

Doris gave me her hand and we walked the rest of the way home. I believe life offers perfect moments, if we are aware enough to recognize them. Walking home from the Rutland Fair on a cold night in September of 1960 with Doris was one such perfect moment for me.

When I got home to Connecticut the next day, I went right to my room and wrote a letter to Doris. To this day I remember her address in Rutland, Vermont—it was 84 Plain Street.

A few days later I received a letter from her. Could this really be happening to me? At age 16 is it possible that the boy with average looks, average grades ,and a big mouth could win the best young lady on the face of the earth? It sure seemed possible in mid-September 1960.

We exchanged four more letters and arranged to have a second and third date on homecoming weekend at Doris' high school in Rutland.

It was now early October, the most beautiful season of the year in Vermont. I drove north with my mom, who would spend time visiting her parents and sister in Rutland while I went to a weekend's worth of events with Doris.

I walked from my grandfather's house on Meadow Street to the high school for the football game against Brattleboro and arrived there towards the end of the game. Mt. St. Joseph won, and all the kids and parents were walking out of the stadium in what looked like a victory parade. I recall the students chanting "We beat Brattleboro." It was a happy scene with one glaring exception. I was supposed to meet Doris after the game, but she wasn't at the meeting place we'd agreed upon.

I'd just received a letter from her the day before driving to Vermont saying how excited she was to see me. It reminded me of the movie *Casablanca* and the scene at the train station in Paris where Humphrey Bogart playing "Rick" was supposed to meet "Ilsa," played by Ingrid Bergman. She'd changed her plans at the last minute and left Rick standing in the rain.

A bit dramatic maybe, but that's how I felt. A few minutes later I caught up with Doris in the parade and tried to walk with her, but she hurried ahead with her friends, barely even saying hello. Now I was hurt and confused.

I knew I still had a date with her for the next night so I walked back to my grandparents' house thinking all would be well by morning.

As I was getting dressed for the dance at the high school the phone rang. It was Doris' friend Betty saying Doris couldn't go to the dance. There was no further explanation. I was confused and hurt at the same time, and I kept thinking about the letter I'd received just two days earlier. What could possibly have happened in the span of 24 hours that would change someone's feelings that much?

I hardly slept that Saturday night since Doris and I had not spoken or made any plans for Sunday. By noon my mom and I would need to begin the drive south to Connecticut. Around 10 a.m. I couldn't stand it any longer. I called my cousin Janie and asked her if she could at least arrange a meeting with Doris so I could get an explanation. She called back and said, "Meet Doris at Betty's house at 11 a.m." I felt a sense of relief that I would at least get some kind of clarity.

I drove to Betty's house and found Doris and Betty sitting on the front porch. Doris seemed like she'd never seen me before, but she was polite and explained that her father didn't want her dating someone from another state. She also said she couldn't write to me anymore. There was nothing I could do; it was all over.

I drove home to Connecticut in silence, wondering what had happened. How it could hurt so much, especially since we'd only had one date on one evening?

Over the next few weeks, thanks to my friends at my high school, I slowly began to recover from the first real heartbreak of my life. Then I got a letter from Betty and the whole mystery was cleared up.

She told me that Doris really did like me at first, but that she'd also liked another boy during the summer who never paid any attention to her: that is, until two days before I returned to Vermont for our weekend together. The letter she'd written saying how excited she was to see me apparently arrived in my mailbox a couple of days after the guy she liked before me, started to notice her. I never blamed her; it could happen to anyone. But it did hurt.

In the months and years that followed I rebounded nicely with friends and girlfriends and even more trips to the Rutland Fair, but 1960 would be a turning point in my life. I got my driver's license, the Yankees lost a heartbreaker to the Pirates, JFK was elected president, and in a very special way I lost Anthony forever.

A Reason to Smile

Recently I contacted my Vermont cousin Janie, now living in Maryland. She called Doris and we've all been exchanging letters, emails and texts. They were good friends all through school and I'm happy this book helped bring them closer again. Who knows, maybe we'll all meet at the Rutland Fair and go on some rides.

CHAPTER FIVE

In the Army Now

"We'll be firing tracer bullets and real bullets just a few inches
above ground. If you stand up you will be shot."
– Drill Sergeant- Fort Jackson, S.C. 1964

O f all the things I heard in my ten weeks at Fort Jackson, South Carolina, that was the one statement that stuck in my memory all these years.
It was a few days before our final test at Army basic training. It was called the infiltration course and was designed to emulate the Allied invasion of Normandy 20 years earlier, in June of 1944. Before I go any further, let me be clear about one thing. Any comparison to real combat and certainly to D-Day would be an insult to the thousands of soldiers and Marines who didn't return from war, but at the time our drill sergeants were trying to keep us focused so we would do the right thing.

In December of 1963 I was in my first year at Wright Technical School in Stamford, Connecticut, studying to be an electrician. For a kid already licensed as a barber and working in his dad's shop five days a week, why would I be in school learning how to wire a house?

Good question. Here's the answer. Dad wanted me to learn a second trade. He already knew I wanted to be a radio broadcaster. I'd already visited my Uncle Ralph in upstate New York and was already hooked, but my dad wanted me to have a second back-up career in case that crazy idea of show business didn't work out.

I might have been a class cutup, a real daydreamer who could imagine myself in almost any situation, but I did respect my dad and I didn't want to hurt his feelings. Besides, he was probably right. If I had stayed at Wright Tech the entire two years, I'd be able to fix my front doorbell today without shocking myself.

As much respect as I had for Dad I quickly lost interest in trade school, and on a Friday afternoon in late December I stopped off at an Army recruiting office to enlist.

Keep in mind that this was one month after the assassination of President Kennedy. And the new president, Lyndon Johnson, had already decided to send more troops to South Viet Nam and stepup the fight against the Viet Cong.

The draft was very much in effect in those days, so to avoid being drafted I decided to enlist for three years. I'd been told by friends that enlisting would give me a better chance to choose my M.O.S., the Army acronym for Military Occupational Specialty.

It was just before 5 p.m. when I stepped into the recruiting office. The sergeant on duty welcomed me, listened to my request to enlist, and then told me to come back on Monday since he was closing the office for the weekend.

Two days later, on Sunday, my brother Phil and wife Fran came to my parents' house for dinner, and I mentioned that I was going to enlist the next day. I'll never forget my brother's reaction. "Wait a minute, why are you doing that? Why don't you join the Army Reserves instead? You serve six months active duty and five and a half years reserve duty. If you like it that much I'm sure you can enlist then." It made sense to me since it was coming from my brother who had served in Germany as an Army medic a few years earlier.

So, the next day I drove to Danbury and signed up with the 318th Signal battalion for a six-year term in the reserves. I would attend weekly meetings at the reserve center until late March, then report to Fort Jackson, South Carolina, for basic training.

Train Ride

Early on the morning of March 26 my dad and brother dropped me off at the Bridgeport train station for the 24-hour trip to Columbia, South Carolina. I'd never set foot out of New England in the first 19 years of my life, so South Carolina may as well have been a foreign country.

The train ride was an adventure in itself. About a dozen other guys boarded with me in Bridgeport and once it was clear we were all headed into the Army, we bonded fairly quickly. It was my first exposure to guys from completely different backgrounds than me. Bridgeport is a big city compared to Wilton. As much as we were taught to love and respect individuals of all races and backgrounds, the truth is, my exposure during my school years was quite limited.

What made it even more interesting is that the train stopped in New York City to pick up another hundred or so recruits, so the trip from there to South Carolina took on some really interesting twists.

I got a kick out of some of the guys from New York, many of whom being pretty vocal about what they expected in the Army. Or course nobody really knew what to expect, but it was interesting and kind of funny to listen to the guys who thought they did.

Since it was a 24-hour trip we stayed in Pullman cars in bunk-style beds with curtains across the front. I didn't sleep well the first night, my mind swirling with anticipation about the next day. At one point early in the morning, I remember an African-American porter teasing some of us about our destination. He didn't say much about the Army, but he did warn us that the snakes in South Carolina were huge and very aggressive. Thanks, buddy.

Next Stop, Columbia

"Next stop, Columbia," the porter announced as we all lined up to get off the train, with absolutely no idea what to expect.

We were met by a dozen or so uniformed Army sergeants and corporals who directed us from the train to waiting buses. There was no yelling, just clear, sharply stated instructions on which bus to board. At this point I was feeling pretty good about my time in the Army. That was about to change.

Welcome to Fort Jackson

About 15 minutes after leaving the station we began to see signs of a large military base. Acre after acre of wooded land followed by open fields, some with platoons of soldiers in fatigue uniforms marching or jogging. The military term for jogging in those days was "double time," something I heard on a regular basis in the coming weeks.

Off in the distance, small weapons fire could be heard from one of the many firing ranges at Fort Jackson. I would find out soon that 35,000 young men were involved in various stages of basic training that summer at Fort Jackson.

Soon we began to see building after building of the same color and design. It was clear that those were the barracks, one of which would become my home for the next eight weeks.

Just as I was starting to feel like this whole basic training thing wouldn't be too tough to handle, the buses pulled in front of one of the barracks and I began to hear shouting. At first I thought a fight had broken out in front of the bus. Quickly I realized that the shouting was coming from a drill sergeant just outside the door of the bus. "Get off that bus you scums, you losers, you momma's boys! This ain't summer camp; you're in the Army now." We scrambled for the door and were immediately lined up in front of one of the barracks. "Now, get inside, and find a bunk. Find a bunk! What's wrong with you morons!? I can't believe we have to train this bunch of idiots."

Full disclosure here, the language was much worse than I just described, but there's really no point in going there. I will say this much, in all my years at a small-town high school in Wilton, Conn., I don't recall hearing the F-word more than a few times, and I never said the word. It just wasn't a word used much in the 50s or the 60s in southern New England. Oh, I heard swear words or cuss words as they were once called, but I didn't use them much.

My own dad had a full and separate vocabulary of language he used when he was mad. His favorite for me was, "You dizzy bastard." I'm pretty sure he knew I wasn't an actual bastard, but I must admit at times he did think I was a little "dizzy" or "off beat," to use a different term. Let's face it, any kid who hit rocks into the woods while calling play-by-play of an imaginary ballgame could probably be described as a little "dizzy." The only time Dad used that term on me was when I did something without thinking. Like the time he asked me to remove the snow chains from the back wheels of his old Plymouth and I somehow managed to get them caught in the brake linings. Or the time I got a new bow and arrow set for Christmas and within minutes shot out a window in the garage.

Years later, when we were both much older, my dad told me he never really meant to call me names and when he did he was just trying to teach me the right thing to do. I'm so glad he told me that, otherwise the title of this book might have been, *Memoirs of a Dizzy Bastard*.

As we scrambled into the barracks to find a bunk I quickly realized there was no assigned sleeping like a kid would find at summer camp. It was literally every man for himself.

I ran from one bunk to another until I found one with no one standing next to it. I grabbed a lower bunk and just stood there waiting for further instructions. "Attention!" yelled one of the drill sergeants. Luckily, in my few months of reserve training in Connecticut, I knew how to stand at attention and keep my mouth shut.

For the next ten minutes, between insults featuring far worse labels than "dizzy bastard," we stood at attention, trying to sort out all that the drill sergeants were explaining to us.

"You'll line up outside the barracks and be taken for haircuts, then to supply for duffel bags and uniforms, then back here for more instructions. Do you understand that?"

"Yes sir!" we said, to which the sergeant screamed, "You idiots, do not address me as sir! I am a sergeant. You will address me with, 'Yes, sergeant.'" "Yes, sergeant," we replied. "I can't hear you," he snapped back, to which we in full voice answered, "Yes, sergeant!"

As I got into line for the camp barber shop I remember thinking to myself, "this is a little scary, but I'll get used to it." I was right on both counts.

Army Barber

There were at least 75 of us in line for haircuts as we stood outside the small base barber shop. I remember walking to the front of the line to see how many barbers would be doing the work. Of course "the work" wasn't exactly a style cut with a scalp massage and hot lather razor finish, but I was still curious about the barbers.

I was shocked when I walked into the shop and saw six chairs and only one barber. Without asking my platoon sergeant I walked up to the barber and said,

"I have a barber's license, can I help you?" He was a little stunned, but quickly said, "Sure, take the next chair and get to work."

So, my first official—or shall we say unofficial—job in the military was cutting every stitch of hair off of the same recruits I'd been herded off the bus with just a few hours earlier. Here's the best part of all: The sergeant in charge of my group of recruits didn't even notice that I'd stepped out of line and was now one of the barbers. Only when we finished the last recruit did he do a double-take when he looked at me and yelled, "Hey, how did you get in here? What are you doing?" The barber on duty explained that thanks to me the line moved twice as fast and the sergeant just grunted and mumbled, "All right, get outside, get in line. We're heading over to supply."

Suddenly on the first day of basic training I had my confidence back. I also had a couple dozen new customers for later haircuts, for a dollar each. I was the only guy in the barracks with cash in my pocket all the time.

For the next two weeks we got yelled at just about all day long. We were taken out on long marches, most in double time, put through drills and physical training and learned some basics about folding socks and underwear and making beds so tight you could bounce a quarter off them. The only frustrating thing about those first two weeks is that they didn't count towards the eight weeks of basic training. We were officially in a holding unit since the actual training battalions were already at full capacity.

Easter Sunday

I'll never forget my first holiday away from home. My family spent all the major holidays together so I felt pretty lonely standing in a line of 20 recruits waiting to use the same pay phone on Easter Sunday morning. Once I got on the phone I had a few minutes to say hi to everyone before yielding to the next guy in line. I have so much respect for the men and women who spent multiple holidays away from home in the military, thousands of them in combat situations. My little bout of loneliness was nothing compared to what they must have felt.

Escalation

I didn't have a lot of political savvy in those days, otherwise I would've been able to sense that something was amiss. As I look back now I realize that President Johnson was getting ready to ramp-up our American presence in Viet Nam. In early 1964 we had fewer than 25,000 U.S. troops in there. By the time I was discharged from the service in 1970, 335,790 American military were serving in the Viet Nam war.

Basic Training

At the end of the two weeks, we were taken by bus to another part of Fort Jackson to begin formal basic training. We were already used to the screaming insults from our sergeants and now anticipated a physical challenge to go along with it.

I'll never forget getting off the bus at my new barracks and hearing the gentle, controlled voice of my new unit leader, Sgt. Sevedra. He was a Hispanic man about 5'5" tall with combat boots so well-polished you could see your own image in them. In those days Army fatigues or work uniforms were olive drab green. The camos only came about during our actions in the Middle East in 2002; prior to that it was olive drab all the way. The sergeant's uniform was perfectly pressed. At first I didn't realize Sgt. Sevedra would be with us for the entire eight weeks of training. I was certain that the Army put this soft-spoken man in charge of us for the first hour only to replace him with a cadre of screamers for the rest of training.

As it turned out the sergeant was tough on us physically but gained our respect in those first few days by letting us know exactly what was expected of us. I learned quickly enough that even the military had different types of leaders whose styles ran the spectrum from outward and animated to reserved and detailed.

Each week our training camp added a new layer to what we'd learned earlier. From cleaning an M-14 rifle to scaling a 12-foot wall or crossing a 50-foot wide, 15-foot deep ditch on a log meant to resemble a fallen tree.

Army Hospital

I actually ended up in the base hospital for two weeks, not with an injury caused by some heroic event but with an infection caused by my combat boots. The back of my left boot kept rubbing my Achilles tendon until it broke through the skin, and made a hole the size of a dime. It quickly became infected.

I spent four days in the infirmary on penicillin before rejoining my unit in time to try and qualify for a medal in rifle training. Somehow, with a little luck and some memory of shooting my dad's shotgun years earlier, I qualified for a sharpshooter medal. I was feeling pretty good about myself a week or so later when I came down with the measles.

I was back in the hospital for two days when my platoon sergeant informed me that if I didn't get back to my unit in the next 48 hours I'd have to recycle to the next training unit and do the eight weeks all over again.

I promised him I'd be out in time even though I had no idea how I was going to do it. Then it came to me. Since a very busy nurse would probably be the one inspecting me for spots on my face and body maybe I could take baby powder and put it on my chest just before the exam. It worked. I covered the few red blotches on my body with powder and the nurse, who was overworked anyway and probably tired of my wisecracks every day, put a flashlight up to my chest, stepped back and said, "Okay, you're clear. Get out of here."

Two weeks later I graduated from basic training and was headed back home for two weeks leave.

Fort Stewart

On June 18, 1964 I celebrated my 20th birthday on a train. I'd finished two weeks leave and was headed for Fort Stewart in Hinesville, Georgia. I would spend the next five months there learning about military communications, and getting an instant education into the differences between my home in New England and the Deep South.

My haircutting skills immediately came in handy in my new barracks. I offered pre-inspection haircuts for one dollar and that added up to an extra 20 bucks in my pocket every two weeks. For a private first class in the U.S. Army making $76.00 a month, an extra $40.00 was a luxury.

Boxing Friend

Probably my biggest adjustment in the Army was getting used to all the drinking. Every two weeks most of the guys in my barracks went into town and got drunk on pay day. I never saw the point in it and instead would go over to the base gym and bang on the heavy punching bag for an hour or so a couple times a week. That's when I became friends with a guy named Ardian Farinas, an Army boxing champion. We hung out together for the next five months and even double-dated a few times to the local drive-in.

Transportation

A few months before joining the Army I saved up some money and bought a car. As crazy as it seems, I bought a new Plymouth Valiant convertible for $2100 from a dealership in Stamford, Conn. After a few weeks at Fort Stewart I took the train home and drove my car back to the base with a friend named Harold Swanson from New York City. We drove for 17 hours without stopping, getting back to the base in plenty of time for the next day's inspection. Having a car parked outside the barracks was a blessing and a curse. I could go anywhere I wanted with a two-day weekend pass and get dates with some of the girls in town, but I also became a taxi driver for any friends who also wanted to get to town.

LBJ Sticker

My first experience in cultural shock came a few days after I started driving into Hinesville for stops at the grocery store or the "Pigadilly," a drive-in featuring barbecue burgers and pretty southern girls on roller skates. Two of my best friends in the barracks were African-American. Make no mistake about it, racism was alive and well in my home state of Connecticut, but it was subtle and unnoticed by most white people.

In the south it was right out there in front of us. On many occasions we had to forego eating breakfast at a local diner because of a sign outside that clearly said, "No Colored."

One day on my way back from flirting with a waitress named Linda at the local movie theater, I was pulled over by a Georgia state trooper. He walked over to my car and politely said, "Soldier, you weren't doing anything wrong, but I thought I should warn you about something." "Yes, sir," I answered. He pointed to my rear bumper and said, "For your own good I'd take that LBJ sticker off my car. This isn't Connecticut," he said. "Not many LBJ fans down here."

———•———

This was the summer of 1964, when Johnson, who had replaced John F. Kennedy in November of 1963 after the assassination, was running for re-election against Barry Goldwater. "I'll take your advice," I told the officer, not wanting any trouble, especially that far from home. When I got back to the barracks I used a razor blade and removed the bumper sticker.

In November of that year LBJ won re-election by a landslide. He lost only four states. Georgia was one of them.

Bye Bye Birdie

One benefit to having my car at the base was dating. I saw three different girls in my five months in Georgia. The first was Linda. She was very friendly, had an alluring southern accent, and quickly accepted my invitation to the drive-in. The movie showing in the summer of 1964 was *Bye Bye Birdie,* starring Ann-Margret, Janet Leigh, Dick Van Dyke, Paul Lynde, Ed Sullivan and Bobby Rydell. When I say the summer of '64 I mean the entire summer. I swear that movie ran for two months. Linda and I saw it three times.

I also found a local church to my liking and met a girl there. We saw *Bye Bye Birdie* once as well. Then I met the daughter of one of the base colonels. He wasn't at the top of the command, but he was close. I'll never forget driving to the colonel's house to pick up his daughter. He smiled politely and shook my hand. As I walked to the car with my date, the colonel's wife walked with us. She came around to the driver's side, looked me in the eye with a smile and said, "Have a good time. Have her home by 11, and don't you touch one hair on my daughter's body."

Now, I was pretty polite to begin with, if I do say so, but that night at the drive-in, watching *Bye Bye Birdie* for my fourth time, I didn't come to within two feet of that girl. It got so bad that at one point she said, "Don't you like me?" I said, "Yes, I like you, but I can't get your mom's image or voice out of my head." She laughed and we had a good time. We even dated a couple more times before the end of my time at Fort Stewart.

By the end of the summer of 1964 I'd visited the Pigadilly Drive-in seven times, went to church five times, hit the heavy bag at the gym 11 times, and could recite the entire script from *Bye Bye Birdie*.

I dated Linda, Melody and Caroline all while falling for Kim McAfee, the character played by Ann-Margret in *Bye Bye Birdie*.

A Reason to Smile

I found the old DVD of *Bye Bye Birdie* and watched it the other night. I still know the words to most of the songs and a good portion of the speaking parts.

CHAPTER SIX

Portrait of a Champion

"Your talent is God's gift to you.
What you do with it is your gift back to God."
– Leo Buscaglia

I f you could choose to be great at anything, what would it be? Would you be a great singer, pianist, golfer, actor, athlete, writer, poet or artist? I realize you can't wish one of those talents on yourself and even if you do have natural ability in one of those areas, you'll still need hard work, perseverance and passion to reach your goal.

Topping my list would be singing and playing piano. In fact I'm singing as I'm writing this so it's a good thing you're not here. I mean how many times can you sing "Runnin Bear and Little White Dove" before everyone leaves the room?

Without exception, all the experts I know in every field of endeavor have combined all the qualities listed above to become exceptional in their chosen fields. So what sets them apart? What makes them a champion in their chosen field? In my opinion it's the sharing of those talents for the benefit of others.

One such person is portrait artist Michael Reagan. I met Michael in the early 1980s when I was sports director at KING-5 television. He presented me with a portrait of myself in a beautiful frame. Don't judge here, but I wrapped in up and gave it to my mom for Mother's Day. She cherished it for the rest of her life.

———

Over the years I'd see Michael occasionally at a sports dinner or benefit auction. Every time I ran into him he was offering a portrait of a local athlete like Edgar Martinez or Steve Largent to raise money for a local cause. Michael would draw two portraits of the celebrity, giving them one and asking them to autograph the second one. Then he donated that second drawing to local fund-raisers.

His first such drawing featured Warren Moon, who had starred at quarterback for the University of Washington Huskies in the late 1970s, and later the Houston Oilers and Seattle Seahawks of the NFL. Moon was inducted into the Pro Football Hall of Fame in 2006. Moon donated that portrait to the Fellowship of Christian Athletes fundraiser. It fetched $1800.

Michael grew up in Seattle and graduated from Lincoln High School in 1965. Shortly afterwards, a childhood friend was killed in Viet Nam. Immediately following the funeral service, Mike joined the service along with three other childhood buddies. Two of them joined the Army while Mike and another friend enlisted in the Marine Corps.

Within a few months Michael joined the war effort in Viet Nam. Combat has been described by many as long periods of down time interrupted by short spurts of terrifying chaos. During that down time Michael often drew portraits of his fellow Marines. In some cases those images were all that returned home.

Like so many men who saw combat, Mike witnessed death firsthand, on two occasions holding friends in his arms as they died. When he returned home from the war in April of 1968, he wondered why he was spared. It would be years before Mike had a clear answer.

In between dealing with the dark images of war etched in his memory, Mike found solace in drawing portraits of friends and relatives.

A friend saw a portrait of Katharine Hepburn Mike had finished and encouraged him to pursue a career as an artist. While driving a truck and working as a furniture salesman, Mike enrolled in the Brunley School of Professional Art, now known as the Art Institute.

———

Throughout our lives there are magic moments and encounters that can become landmarks of success for us. More often than not, we don't appreciate those moments immediately and often don't recognize them at all until much later in life.

One such moment for Michael Reagan came when he met actor Van Johnson backstage during a live theatre event in Seattle. Showing gratitude for Johnson's treatment of his friends and family, Michael drew a pencil portrait and presented it to the actor.

That opened the floodgate to more than 1500 celebrity portraits drawn by Reagan over the years.

By the mid-1980s his drawings of sports celebrities became a mainstay in the Seattle charity auction community.

All the major benefit auctions in the Seattle area included at least one and often multiple Mike Reagan portraits.

 Seattle Mariner star Edgar Martinez purchased a lithograph of President George H.W. Bush and First Lady Barbara Bush for $12,500 at an auction for Seattle Children's Hospital.

An original portrait of Harrison Ford was sold at the Museum of Flight in Seattle for $7,500. Michael's collection includes such notables as Bob Hope, Katharine Hepburn, Audrey Hepburn, Red Skelton and Ingrid Bergman. He's also drawn portraits of every Heisman Trophy winner and most NFL Hall of Fame members.

In fact, over the years Reagan's celebrity and sports portraits have raised well over $10 million for various organizations across the country.

For most of us, that would be enough of a legacy to keep our chests puffed out for years. It was not enough for Michael. Sure, his talent made him famous throughout the country and he had no problem earning money from it, but there was one piece still missing.

"There are fewer than 10 people in my life that if any one of them had not appeared when they did, I wouldn't be doing what I'm doing," Mike told me recently.

One of those people is former President George W. Bush who met with Michael in 2002 to accept a gift portrait of his wife, Laura. "You've done a beautiful job capturing her eyes," the President told him. "I'm going to hang this portrait in the Oval Office so I can see it every day."

Early in 2003 KING-5, the local NBC affiliate in Seattle, did a feature piece on Michael's career which included a five-year stint working for *Playboy* magazine. As he tells it, "one of the playmates commented on my work and that got the attention of a woman in Boise, Idaho."

The next day, Cherise Johnson called Michael and asked what he would charge to do a portrait of her husband. "I thought I was about to get rich," Michael said "and then she told me her husband was a Corpsman, killed in action in Iraq a year earlier.

"Corpsman are among the bravest people I've ever met," Michael told her. "Send me a photo of your husband and I'll do his portrait no charge."

Little did he know at the time but the now-famous Fallen Heroes Project was born that day. Since then, Michael has drawn over 5000 portraits of fallen heroes for families, never charging a single dime for any of them.

Sandy Hook

"There's a spiritual component to my project, it can't be denied anymore," Michael told me. "I've been doing this for 14 years. I gave up my life for this. One day I was in my office drawing a portrait of a soldier killed in action. My wife, Cheryl, came in from upstairs and told me to turn on the television. 'Something has happened at a school in Newtown, Connecticut,' she told me."

As they watched the horrible news from Sandy Hook school unfold Michael felt sick, angry and helpless.

The next day he began getting phone calls from friends, mostly Goldstar parents for whom he had done portraits. They were calling from Connecticut, New Jersey, New York, Vermont, all around New England, all asking Michael's help. "What can you do for these families?" they asked.

Michael was stuck. He didn't want to be the intruder calling families across the country to offer portraits of victims. This is where the spiritual component appears again in this story.

The next day Michael received a Christmas card from his friend Chris Burns of Shelton, Connecticut, just a few miles from Newtown. "I called him right away," Michael said "Chris, I'd like to help, but I don't know where to start. I'm getting calls from families."

"All the interaction is going through Pat Llodra, the Mayor of Newtown, and she's a good family friend," Chris said. "I'll call her tonight."

The next day Mayor Llodra sent letters to each family affected by the tragedy offering Michael's services as a portrait artist.

Michael began getting phone calls from the families within a few days. He asked each for a photo of the family member killed in the shooting. "Six weeks later every family had their portrait. We even connected with a framer I'd worked with before on some soldiers' portraits. It all worked out.

"God has given me a gift," Michael always says. "I hope I'm doing what I'm supposed to be doing with it."

Reason to Smile

Last Christmas I wrote a Facebook post about my sister Bunny who died at age 10 a few months after Christmas in 1956. It was about our last Christmas together and in fact appears in full in this book. Michael saw the post and called me the next day asking for a photo of Bunny. I only had a few, but sent him my best one. The breathtaking portrait of my sister Bunny appears in this chapter. Michael's gift has warmed the hearts of families around the world, including my own.

CHAPTER SEVEN

A Glance at Sports

"Choose a job you love
and you'll never have to work a day in your life."

I t's 6:15, time for a glance at sports." That was my simple, concise introduction
every hour, at 15 after the hour, eight hours a day, from the summer of
1971 until the spring of 1975 on WMMM radio in Westport, Conn. It was
unheard-of in those days to do a sports report every hour all day long, but that's
what my new boss, Bob Roberts, wanted.

His real name was Robert Doliche. He had a classic radio announcer's voice
and wore a suit to work every day. He lived in New York City and made the
reverse commute every day to Westport to run the small AM/FM station. Bob
taught me more about broadcasting in those four years than I could've learned
in a lifetime.

This was not my first radio job, not by a longshot. That happened in 1970,
when I got a tip from a disc jockey friend of mine who worked at WLAD in
Danbury. "There's a small station in Brookfield, WINE radio, looking for a
Sunday night board operator. You should apply, but it probably doesn't pay
much." That was certainly not an exaggeration.

At the time, I was operating a barber shop in Wilton, Conn. while also writing
and editing the sports section of the *Wilton Bulletin* weekly newspaper. I made
the 25-mile drive to Brookfield, applied for the job and nailed it. Forget that it
was the Sunday night shift from 4 p.m. to midnight and only paid two dollars an
hour; I was a professional radio broadcaster.

Run My Commercial

I ran the board and read "live" commercials and public service announcements for eight hours a night. In between those duties I also played music, known at the time as "easy listening," or "elevator" music. The station also carried New York Mets games live, an oldies record show with a host named Will Anderson, and the Portuguese Hour. I had to be on my toes for commercial breaks for eight hours every Sunday night.

One Sunday around 6:15 in the evening the studio phone rang. You see, I also had to answer all phones of which there were very few, thank goodness. I answered the phone professionally. "WINE radio, this is Tony." On the other end of the line was a listener who was also a sponsor. "Hey, Tony, can you do me a favor? I've got some friends over tonight and they'd like to hear my radio commercial. Would you mind playing it?"

In today's world of automated programming that type of request would never get consideration. In fact, you can't even call a radio station on the weekends now; there's nobody there.

In this case I figured the guy was a good customer, so I told him to wait until the next song ended and I'd play his commercial. I'm sure I broke some sort of FCC rule, but since nobody complained about it I wasn't worried.

After a few months at WINE I decided to make an audio tape and take it around to some of the other radio stations in the area.

I lived in the small town of Wilton and was already writing for the *Wilton Bulletin* weekly newspaper, so I thought it would be a natural to create a radio show about the local high school team, Little League and other youth sports activities. I called it the "Wilton Sports Spotlight." I even went out and got two sponsors for the show to make it more attractive to the radio stations.

Rejected

The program director was a nice enough guy named Dick, also known for his local sports reports and play-by-play of high school football games. His claim to fame in my book was his call of the 1952 Little League World Series. Founded in 1947, the World Series in 2017 marks the 70th year of that event in Williamsport, Pennsylvania.

In 1952, Norwalk, Conn. beat Monongahela, Penn. 4-3 in the championship game, thanks in part to the Dimiglio brothers.

Now, here I was almost 20 years later at WNLK, asking for a job as a radio sportscaster. Dick was very courteous, took my tape reel, put it on his machine and played it back. After about a minute, he took the reel off, handed it back to me and said, "Very nice, Tony, but not quite polished enough for us. Please work on it and come back in six months."

I thanked him and walked out the door to my car. After a few minutes of feeling sorry for myself, I drove back through downtown Norwalk to the Post Road and on into Westport.

WMMM

Westport had two radio stations owned by a man named Donald Flamm. They were together in a building on Main Street, next to Oscar's Deli which, by the way, is still in business today. The AM station was called WMMM while the FM was WDJF, the initials of the owner.

I went to the front desk and asked to see the general manager. As I sat in the lobby, just the smell of the inside of the building got me excited. It smelled like a radio station. I could see the big glass window of the AM studio from the lobby. Behind the window sat a man in his mid-50s sorting through records. Occasionally the "on air" light would go on and I'd hear him say, "This is WMMM in Westport, Connecticut." I could imagine myself in that role, but I didn't want to get ahead of myself. After all, I'd already been rejected once that day. This was another longshot, but I had to take it.

After a few minutes Bob Roberts walked into the lobby, reached out to shake my hand and said, "Welcome to WMMM, what can I do for you?"

"Thanks for seeing me, Mr. Roberts. I brought in a demo tape and would appreciate if you'd listen to it." At that point any reply would not have been a surprise to me. He could've said, no thanks, we don't need anyone, or come back next week or don't come at all.

Instead, he said, "Follow me." We went into an empty studio, he placed the reel on a huge tape player built into the wall and hit the play button.

After about 30 seconds he stopped the tape and I assumed that my radio career would go down in history as over and out, just like that. I was wrong.

"I like this," he said. "You have a nice voice for sports." Then he said something I didn't expect. "I like your idea of a sports show about Wilton. We've been trying to get more listeners from that town, and this might help. When can you start the show?" I was stunned, but immediately said, "I can start it this coming Saturday."

Wilton Sports Spotlight

So began a two-year run of the Wilton Sports Spotlight on WMMM in Westport, Conn. The show was sponsored by Bonanza Steak House and Mohawk Motors. My weekly profit for the Wilton Sports Spotlight was $35.00.

After the show was on the air for two weeks I got a call from Bob in my barber shop. "Tony, I'd like to meet with you about an idea I have, can you come to Westport?" I put a small "Back in an Hour" sign on my shop door and drove to WMMM. At this point my heart was pounding. My radio career was about to take a sharp turn upward, thanks to Bob Roberts and WMMM.

Me,
Bob Roberts –
WMMM Radio

"Have you ever done play-by-play?" Bob asked at our meeting.

"I have done a little and would love the chance to do more," I told him.

Thank goodness he didn't ask me for a tape since none existed. I had a sense that he knew that because he said, "Tony, I'll tell you what, there's a high school all-star football game next month in Bridgeport. I want you to go to the game with a portable tape recorder, do play-by-play, and bring it back to me. I also have another guy, his name is Bob Strong. He's also interested in doing radio sports. You guys will do the game on the same recorder, one do play-by-play the other color for a half, then reverse it in the second half. Once I hear the tape I'll determine which of you guys will call the game and which will be the color commentator."

We had a second meeting a few days later so I could actually meet the guy I was competing against for the job, and then we traveled together to the game on a warm August night.

I called the first half and Bob called the second half. The game ended in a scoreless tie. We decided to flip a coin to see who would call the plays in overtime. I won the toss.

My fate was decided almost immediately when the East all-star team ran the overtime kickoff back for a touchdown to win the game. The call of that play got me the job as the play-by-play man for Staples High School football on WMMM.

For the next four years I worked side by side with Bob Strong doing football and basketball broadcasts. We even did the Staples High School softball games during the state tournament one year and the Little League World Series when Westport made the state finals. We had a blast.

Bob Roberts became a mentor for both of us. He took us to baseball games in New York, a boxing match at Madison Square Garden, and he attended every local broadcast with us, acting as producer and director. He was like another dad to both of us.

ESPN

One of our football sponsors was the Peppermill Steak House in Westport. Bob would take us to lunch frequently to critique our work and go over the upcoming schedule. I remember one day in a quiet voice Bob told us, "I've always had a dream to create a radio and television station that would broadcast only sports, all day long." I admit I rolled my eyes when I heard that, and it wasn't until years later that I realized Bob's reasoning behind an hourly sportscast called "A Glance at Sports" was exactly what helped create ESPN a few miles northeast of Westport in an industrial town called Bristol.

Full-Time Job

A few weeks into my play-by-play career Bob offered us both a job doing sports hourly at WMMM. I worked the morning shift from 6 a.m. until 2 p.m. and Bob Strong worked the afternoon and evening shifts. We were paid $125 a week plus $65 each for football and another $15 for the football postgame show. That's when I made the bold and somewhat crazy decision to close my barber shop and pursue radio full-time.

Divine Intervention

I've often said that my little sister Bunny, who passed away when she was 10 and I was 11, has always been my guardian angel. There are countless examples of things that have happened to me that could not have been possible without divine help.

I had a year left on my lease at the Village Barber Shop in Wilton when I decided to go into radio full-time. I opted to go to my landlord, Ralph Piersall, owner of the Village Market, to see if I could get out of my lease. My father, who had made his living as a barber, thought I'd lost my mind. "You're going to give up a business to go into radio? That's crazy," he warned me in his very direct manner.

The morning of the day I was going to call my landlord my phone rang. It was the rental agent for the shopping center. Did he get word that I'm about to ask out of my lease, I thought. Holy cow, I'm in trouble now. Before I could say a word he said, "Tony, can you come down to my office in the market? I need to talk to you."

As I walked across the street past Boyd's Toy Store, Stiver's Drugstore and the Center restaurant to the Village Market, I rehearsed what I was going to say to my landlord. Would he charge me a fee for vacating early? Would I be sued? I had no idea.

As I stepped into his office he asked me to close the door. He didn't seem mad at all. In fact, he seemed embarrassed, even a little timid. Then I found out why.

"Tony, I've got bad news. Since your shop is right next to the bank and they've asked for more space to expand their vault, you're going to have to move." I was stunned and thrilled at the same time, but I didn't want to let on until I heard the whole story. "We feel badly that you'll have to close your business, so here's what we're going to do. First, we'll help you find a new location and second, we'd like to return all the rent you've paid us over the first three years of the lease."

I was stunned. I almost fainted on the spot. What did he just say? He's going to return my rent for the past three years? This had to be my sister Bunny pulling strings from heaven, it could have no other explanation.

Granted, I'd only paid a hundred a month for those three years, so my refund would be less than $4000, but it couldn't have come at a better time. I was about to take the job for less than $250 a week in a business that was still new to me with no guarantee for the future. My sister had done it again.

WNLK

A few months later I saw an article in the Norwalk Hour about a young businessman who had just purchased WNLK, the radio station that had rejected me four years earlier. I immediately got in touch with the new owner and offered my services as sports director. Two weeks later, I got the job. The timing was perfect since my first boss and mentor Bob Roberts was about to retire.

For the next two years I worked drive-time sports at WNLK and called play-by-play of Norwalk and Brian McMahon High School sports.

Calvin Murphy

It was during that time that I met Calvin Murphy, one of the most prolific scorers in the history of Norwalk High School, Niagara University and the Houston Rockets. I watched Murphy score 65 points in the state championship basketball game in the mid-1960s. By the time I got to WNLK he was an NBA star but often came back to town for charity events.

On to Television

I made a routine of waking up every morning at 4 a.m. and driving 30 miles from my house in Danbury to WNLK for the morning shift. Toward the end of my second year, a friend who was a writer for WNLK got a job with a television talent agent named Al Primo in Greenwich.

My friend encouraged me to come to his new office and make a video audition tape for a job in television. I had nothing to lose.

The following Monday I drove to Greenwich and with the help of my friend and Mr. Primo we recorded a demo tape. It was a two-minute, ad-libbed commentary about the challenge of driving into the Bronx and parking at Yankee Stadium. The demo had no graphics, was in black and white and wasn't well lit.

None of that mattered since Primo thought it was good enough to get me a job in television. He wasn't a babe in the woods by any stretch. Al Primo is the man who created the tag line "Eyewitness News" for WABC in New York in the early 70s.

Al sent my tape to television stations in Sacramento, Little Rock, Arkansas, and Fort Wayne, Indiana.

Two weeks passed. I heard nothing from any of the stations. Then I got a nice letter of rejection from Sacramento. Cross one off the list. A few days later I got a phone call. "Tony, this is Ian Pearson of WANE TV in Fort Wayne, Indiana. I got your tape and I'd like you to interview for the job as sports director. Can you fly out here next week?" I didn't know what to say; I was stunned. So I said something stupid. "Okay, what airline should I fly? Should I buy my ticket today?" He laughed and said, "No, we buy your ticket; don't worry about it. We'll call you with details."

Three days later, I landed in Fort Wayne. There was one terminal building, so finding Ian Pearson wasn't going to be that difficult. As I walked down the steps of the plane into the terminal a young man in a light-colored suit, wearing western boots and hat, reached out to shake my hand. "I'm Ian Pearson, welcome to Fort Wayne."

As we drove to WANE TV he explained that he'd been in broadcasting right after college but became discouraged and quit, taking a construction job earlier that year. "I was standing in a ditch when I got a call from the general manager of WANE TV. He offered me a job as news director. I took it and here I am."

He told me how the station was trying to modernize its news image by replacing everyone on the evening news at the same time. I was a candidate for sports director.

I did a demo on the set with two other people, met briefly with some of the staff, then took a cab back to my hotel. As I sat in my room that night I wondered how my demo went, how I could've done better. Did I blow it? Did I impress? I might never know.

Keep in mind this was years before cell phones, and I had no way of reaching Ian Pearson to put in a last-minute plug before flying home. So, I did the next-best thing. I took a cab back to WANE late that night and taped a note to Ian on the front door.

Can you imagine doing that today? That note would either be tossed in recycling or taken as evidence by the security guard on-duty.

As it turned out Ian got the note, and I got the job—but not before two long, agonizing weeks of waiting.

Never Give Up

One afternoon I was sitting at my desk at WNLK with a depressed look on my face when Becky, a spirited redhead sales executive, walked by. "Hey, where's that smile?" she said. "You're always so upbeat. What's the problem?" I explained that I'd applied for a job and hadn't heard a word since my trip to Indiana. She looked at me with a smile and said, "No matter what happens, you need to keep the faith. Don't ever give up on your dream."

No more than 15 minutes later my phone rang. It was Ian Pearson. "Tony, we'd like to offer you the job." I was so happy I actually cried for a second. Thank goodness nobody saw me.

Six years after my audio tape was rejected by WNLK I had landed a job in television.

Bittersweet Goodbye

I remember telling Becky I got the job and how happy she seemed. She wished me luck and two weeks later I was on my way to Indiana. A month or so after I was settled in at WANE TV I got a call from the WNLK station manager telling me Becky had died of cancer. She'd known her fate for months, which means she knew she was dying the day she told me, "Don't ever give up on your dream."

Embracing Indiana

Since the state of Indiana was famous for "Hoosier Hysteria," otherwise known as the state high school basketball tournament, I was sure I'd be knee-deep in basketball every winter, but I wanted to do more. I was determined to highlight the sports that got little or no recognition.

My first week on the job I called all ten high schools in Fort Wayne and spoke with the football coaches. I told them I would do a preseason feature on all of them. I still chuckle at the response of one coach whose team was winless the year before. "Why in the world do you want to cover us?" he asked. "Because you just might go 1-9 next season," I told him. We got along great after that.

I had a wonderful four and a half years in Fort Wayne, meeting people I'll never forget. One of those people was a 12-year-old baseball player named Rick Harmann. I've devoted a separate chapter of this book to Rick.

Big Apple Calling

Near the end of my third year at WANE TV I got a call from WNBC in New York. They'd seen a tape of my work and were interested in having me interview for a job as weekend sports anchor. At the time, Marv Albert was sports director along with his duties as play-by-play radio broadcaster with the New York Knicks.

I flew to New York and interviewed with the news director. He liked my tape, but wasn't convinced I'd be tough enough for the number one market in the country. "Will you be able to ask the tough question of a Yankees manager or player? I'm concerned that all of your television experience has been in the 97th market. But we'll let you know."

I returned to Indiana never expecting to hear from WNBC again. I was wrong. A week later I got a call from one of the producers offering to have me sports weekend anchor for one month while still keeping my job in Fort Wayne. "We'll fly you in on Saturday and back home Monday mornings and pay you $500 per day," he told me. Oh my God, I thought, $500 a day. That's a thousand dollars per weekend, nearly as much as I make in a month at WANE TV. I immediately accepted. He told me they would test me for a month and then test another reporter from Chicago for a month before choosing between us.

A few days before my first weekend stint at WNBC he called me back. "Tony, I want to apologize to you. I fully intended to give you a one-month trial, but things have changed since we last talked. Marv's brother Steve has agreed to take the job, and Marv has the last word on the decision." He explained to me that Steve had been offered the job but turned it down, prompting them to call me and the guy in Chicago. What could I say, my chance to do television in New York, where my family and friends could watch me 'live' was dashed because Steve Albert changed his mind. No hard feelings; Steve did a good job.

Divorce

A year later, with my new career in television going well, I lost sight of my most important duty as husband to Molly and father to my children. We never exchanged mean words, but my focus was on myself and my career and not on my family. I was a huge disappointment to my parents, my wife and my children. In June of 1979 Molly and I met with one lawyer and decided to divorce. We agreed that she would move to Portland with the children to be closer to her sister and get a fresh start. It was a heart-wrenching decision for both of us, but that's what we did.

We sold our house, split the money fairly so she could get a head start on a new life and parted ways. I'll never forget June 9, 1979, watching my family drive away to start their journey across the country.

Later that same day, I closed on a smaller house a few blocks from WANE TV. I had signed divorce papers, closed on one house and purchased another on the same day. I remember my real estate agent asking me if I needed a drink. I didn't drink then and I still don't. It's probably just as well. Instead I went for a three-mile run. It was the beginning of a new habit that would sustain me for the remaining year in Fort Wayne and every day since. Running was my escape and still is today.

Tulsa or Seattle

One day, out of the blue, I received an offer to become sports director in Tulsa, Oklahoma.

Just as I was considering the Tulsa job I also got an offer from KOMO in Seattle. And Seattle is only 165 miles north of Portland, where my children now lived.

I had one year remaining on my contract, but since the Tulsa station was owned by Corinthian Broadcasting which also owned WANE TV, the company decided to let me out of the final year of the contract. Easy decision, right? Wrong.

When I went to my management and mentioned the Seattle job they told me I would be sued for breach of contract if I accepted it. They claimed it would present a hardship for them to replace me, not a very solid argument since they'd have to replace me either way. I chose to break my contract and take the Seattle job. They threatened to sue and then an hour later called me in and told me I could go as long as I waited until they found a replacement. I agreed, and a month later I drove my 1979 Chevy Chevelle across the country to Seattle.

My career in Seattle television began officially in August of 1981 as weekend sports anchor on KOMO 4 News. Our news anchor was Steve Pool, who is still at KOMO after more than 40 years.

KOMO 4

I had the privilege of working with some of the most skilled broadcasters and finest human beings one would ever meet in my 14 months at KOMO. Bruce King was my first mentor. He'd enjoyed a long and storied career as a broadcaster in Washington State, as well as a stint in New York at WABC.

Kathy Goertzen was a young college graduate when I met her at KOMO. What a legacy she left for everyone who followed. I became friends with Lori Matsukawa while at KOMO, doing a morning show with her called "Wake Up." Later, we both moved over to KING-5. I spent 11 terrific years there. Lori is still at KING and remains one of the finest anchor-reporters in Seattle television history.

KING 5

On New Year's Day 1982, I started my years at KING-5. I remember anchoring sports that day with Aaron Brown as news anchor. It would be the beginning of a great friendship and winning combination. Aaron, Jean Enersen, Jeff Renner and I earned some of the highest ratings in Seattle television. In all fairness, we didn't have CNN, FOX News or any cable TV competition to contend with in those days. One had to watch either KING or KOMO or KIRO.

KING-5 – Me, Aaron Brown, Jean Enersen, Jeff Renner

We were it.

At KING-5, with Bill Rockey and Dori Monson as producers, we created "Wrestling Hold of the Week," which was a television staple in thousands of households every Wednesday night. I'm pretty sure I wouldn't be allowed to do anything that goofy in today's world of 24-hour "breaking news."

Crime Tape

I'll never forget sitting in with a news consultant in the early 90s at KING-5 and hearing him say, "Television viewers want to see flames and crime tape. That's what attracts viewers, not feel-good stories about a baseball team or a Girl Scouts cookie drive." Then he added, "And in sports, you've gotta show that DUI, that's what draws an audience." I remember thinking how depressing that meeting was. I couldn't wait to get back to my desk and start working on the Wrestling Hold of the Week.

I had wonderful opportunities in my 27 years in Seattle television. I worked side by side with Steve Raible, Susan Hutchison and Harry Wappler at KIRO 7. Even though it was well into the 90s at that point, the news department still allowed me to do some of the fun stuff like "Nosetrodomus" and "Haircut of the Week."

I finished my television career at Q13, doing a morning show with Christine Chen. What started as a feel-good local news-talk show quickly became a more serious "breaking news" program with the onset of Operation Iraqi Freedom in 2003.

I left Q13 in 2004 for a short stint on KIRO radio before catching on as digital media host for the Seattle Seahawks website.

I have only admiration for the young men and women in 21st century television news. It is a tough, daily challenge against corporate ownership and hundreds of competitors large and small, but the people in the Seattle television market do an outstanding job.

A Reason to Smile

I had a blast covering sports in the Seattle area and around the rest of the country, not to mention Olympic Games in Nagano, Japan and Seoul, South Korea and the World Figure-Skating Championships in Helsinki, Finland.

I've covered everything from the National Horse Show at Madison Square Garden to the Seafair hydroplane races in Seattle. Go ahead, ask me to explain the difference between dressage and show jumping, or what boat Chip Hanauer drove before the Miss Budweiser, or which ice skater Rosalynn Sumners dated the year she won the world championship.

CHAPTER EIGHT

Thanks, Doc

"You left me a lot more than I expected."
– Rick Harmann

In the summer of 1980 the United States staged a boycott of the Moscow Olympic Games after the Soviet Union refused to withdraw from Afghanistan. Earlier that year, on May 18, Mount St. Helens erupted, spewing ash across 11 states and five Canadian provinces. Ronald Reagan would win the Republican nomination for President of the United States and run against incumbent Jimmy Carter.

Little did I know that a meeting with a young man named Rick in July of that year would help shape the rest of my life.

I was sports director at WANE TV, the CBS affiliate in Fort Wayne, Indiana. I covered everything from high school basketball to Little League baseball at a time when local television was at its peak.

One night I got a phone call from a Little League volunteer inviting me to the district playoffs later that week, just outside of Fort Wayne. "It's a good tournament, Tony, all by itself. But there's a special reason I think you'll like this story. One of our kids is being honored that night. Please come see us, I think you'll like this story."

The woman sounded so sincere on the phone it was easy for me to agree to cover the story.

The next day photographer Tim Shannon and I made the drive out to the Little League complex not really knowing what to expect. We got there early and the woman on the phone was right there to greet us. "Thanks for coming, you guys. The tall boy over near the bench is named Rick, he's the one being honored tonight. He's one of our best pitchers. Tonight he's throwing out the first pitch."

Now, I know baseball pretty well, and usually your best pitcher starts game one of an elimination series, so I had to ask the obvious question: "Why isn't Rick pitching tonight?"

"Ask him," said the woman.

I didn't see a tall boy near the bench, but I walked over anyway. I did see four or five pre-teen girls huddled around a boy in a wheelchair. One of the girls recognized me and the WANE TV camera and said, "Hey, Rick, you're a star." That's when I realized that Rick was the boy in the wheelchair, and the story became a little clearer though it was still lacking most of the facts.

"Hi, Rick, I'm Tony from Channel 15. Good to meet you," I said.

"I know who you are," he said. "I watch you all the time, well some of the time," he said with a big smile.

"Tell me what's going on, Rick. Why are you being honored tonight? Are you injured? When do you think you'll pitch again?"

I admit I was a little nervous since I didn't know what was going on, but Rick put me at ease with a simple straightforward answer. "I won't be pitching again. I have cancer in my knee; I'm going to have my leg amputated in two weeks."

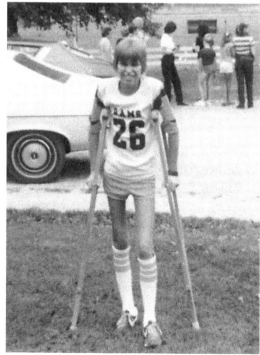

Rick – Indiana, 1980

I was stunned, not to mention embarrassed. Rick saved me again with, "Hey, don't worry about it. You didn't know. Thanks for coming out anyway. These players need the publicity." At that moment I realized this story would be different from any I had covered in the past and would be more than just a 30-second spot on the local news.

After Rick threw out the ceremonial first pitch and the crowd settled back to watch the ballgame, Rick and I went off to the side to do a short interview. He explained that he had felt some pain in his left knee and went to the doctor for a check-up. Tests showed cancer behind the knee cap. It was determined that amputation was necessary to keep the cancer from spreading. As so often happens in life, Rick's father was laid off from his job the same day his son was diagnosed with cancer. This was a horrible time for the family and yet Rick was still smiling.

"Hey, I got a bad break," he said. "It could happen to anybody. All I can do is fight, and I'll beat this thing." I remember thinking, what a wise and mature young man this was standing by me that day and what lessons I might learn from someone 20 years younger than me?

For the next two weeks I visited Rick and his family at their house a number of times. I drove Rick to the mall, took him for milkshakes and burgers, played video games at his house, and prayed with him and his family.

On the day of the surgery I thought about Rick and his family, his mom and dad and two sisters, and how much faith they showed in the days between the diagnosis and the surgery. About 8 p.m. I got a phone call from Rick's mom. "He's out of surgery," she told me in a voice that seemed so tired and stressed all at once. "Rick will call you tomorrow."

Rick did call the next day, saying he was fine and he'd be back home soon. He invited me over. I told him I'd be there. Later that day his mom called me. "Tony, you'll never believe it. Do you know what Rick said when they pulled the sheet back from his leg the morning after the surgery to show him the results? He looked at his leg, now missing below the knee, looked back up at the doctor, smiled and said, "Good job, Doc. You left me a lot more than I expected.""

A year later I accepted a job in Seattle and moved away. Rick and I kept in touch by mail. His mom sent me a videotape of Rick trying to play tackle football in junior high school with one leg. It was nearly impossible, but he did it. He also rode a horse and his motor bike. Early in 1982 I got a call from his dad. "Rick has had a setback, Tony. He's not doing well. He'd love to talk to you." The next voice I heard was Rick's, clearly weakened from fighting for his life. "Hey, Tony, how are you? I just want to tell you thanks for everything. I'll never forget you, same goes for my family. I love you." Through my own tears I managed a weak, "I love you too, Rick, hang in there." Noticing the anguish in my voice, Rick saved me again. "Tony, don't worry about a thing. You're in my will; no money but a nice photo of me in my baseball uniform."

Those were our last words to each other. Rick passed away a few days later, and I attended his funeral in Fort Wayne the following week.

Many years have passed since then. Rick's sister Jeannie got married and had a baby boy a few years later. The boy's name is Rick.

A Reason to Smile

In July and August of every year the district Little League tournaments start. Sometimes I just stop by a game in progress, not even knowing the teams. I love the competition, and I love the game and at the same time watching Little League baseball makes me grateful for meeting Rick and his family all those years ago in Indiana.

CHAPTER NINE

The Seahawks Years

"Talent wins games, but teamwork,
intelligence and grit win championships."

We're pulling the plug on your show." That still ranks as the most direct and honest way I've ever been fired. It wasn't the only time. In fact, it was the second time in a period of nine months.

I was doing a general topic talk show on KIRO radio for three hours on weekday evenings with ratings hovering close to the ground, so the dropping of my show was no surprise.

The program director, Tom Clendenning, had gone out on a limb to give me the opportunity in the first place. I'd met with pretty good success in television sports for 24 years, so the move to talk radio seemed like a safe enough bet. It wasn't, and after nine months the show ended.

To be really effective in news talk radio a couple of elements must exist. First and foremost, the show has to be entertaining. It's almost essential that the host have someone else to bounce ideas off of, keep the pace moving and engage the audience by first engaging each other.

The host doesn't need to be nasty to callers or interview guests but should at least engage them in a way that encourages listeners to stay involved and not tune out.

Too Nice

You were "too nice" to everyone, I was told. You need to have an edge; you need to disagree with callers and guests and shake things up a little. I didn't do that enough and deserved to have my show cancelled.

Now What

After landing the first 10 jobs I applied for in broadcasting I was suddenly zero for two in the space of nine months.

Since it was late September and I was also doing a show called the "Seahawks Huddle," along with the radio postgame show on Sundays, I wasn't completely out in the cold. Then one afternoon at Seahawks headquarters in Kirkland, Vice President of Broadcasting Dave Pearson asked me if I'd help do video interviews on the new Seahawks website. It would involve going to every practice and traveling with the team on the road. I accepted immediately.

I joined veteran sportswriter Mike Kahn on the Seahawks digital media staff and had a very enjoyable 11 years with the team. Mike and I quickly became friends and worked together for three seasons. Then in 2008 Mike got cancer and passed away. He was a good man and a heck of a sportswriter.

Mike Holmgren

In the summer of 1999 I was sports director at KIRO-7, the CBS affiliate in Seattle. One day we got word that the Seahawks had hired Green Bay Packers Super Bowl-winning coach Mike Holmgren. My first opportunity to interview Mike ranks as one of my most enjoyable days in the broadcast business. We set up for a "live shot" at Seahawks headquarters at 11 a.m. for an interview on the noon news.

Just as our news anchor introduced me inside the Seahawks press room, Holmgren walked into the room, shook my hand and the interview began. The timing was perfect. The former Packers coach talked about winning one Super Bowl and almost another, his plans to bring a winner to Seattle and how excited his family was to be back on the West Coast.

There are so many different personalities in coaching, each person approaching the interview process differently. Holmgren had been a high school teacher before going into coaching full-time. He knew how to communicate in a clear and concise way while also entertaining his audience and cleverly avoiding information he didn't want to reveal.

Holmgren ranks in the top five of coaches I've interviewed in my career. Seahawks coach Pete Carroll and Mariners manager Lou Piniella are also in the top five. Okay, fine, I'll reveal the other two coaches on the list: former Notre Dame coach Lou Holtz and former Indiana coach Lee Corso.

Matt Hasselbeck

The Seahawks had finished 8-8 in each of the two seasons before Holmgren appeared on the scene. In his first season they improved to 9-7, dipped to 6-10 in 2000, back to 9-7 in 2001 and 7-9 in 2002.

After spending one season on the Packers' practice squad and two as the back-up for Bret Favre, Matt Hasselbeck was traded to the Seahawks in 2001. He did not enjoy immediate success and, in fact, at one point was replaced as the starter by veteran Trent Dilfer.

Finally, in the 2003 season, Hasselbeck won the job as starter and led the Seahawks to a 10-6 season, their best since 1986.

Two years later, with Hasselbeck at the helm and Shaun Alexander breaking rushing records and an all-pro offensive line, the Seahawks finished 13-3 for the best record in the NFC.

Playoffs

The Seahawks were flying high in the winter of 2005. With a top-seed finish in the regular season Holmgren's potent offense and better-than-average defense would host one and maybe two playoff games.

On January 14, with 67,551 fans packing Qwest Field, the Seahawks knocked off the Washington Redskins 20-10 for their first playoff victory in 21 years.

The following week, 67,837 rocked the stadium while witnessing history. The Seahawks beat the Carolina Panthers 34-14 for the NFC Championship and a spot in the Super Bowl for the first time in franchise history.

Detroit

One common denominator in the first 39 years of Super Bowl championships was their warm weather venue. That changed for Super Bowl XVI, which took place at Detroit's newly minted Ford Field.

———•◆•———

I was still working as a contractor for the team and traveled on one of the staff planes to Detroit on Friday, February 3. When we stepped off the bus in front of the team hotel we received an enthusiastic greeting from Seahawks staff who had arrived in the city the previous Sunday.

I remember visiting the Henry Ford Museum the next day and that was the extent of my leisure time in Detroit.

Super Bowl XVI

The press box at Ford Field was packed beyond capacity. In fact, I didn't have an official seat and had to stand the entire game. I used the opportunity to walk around the stadium, taking notes on the game, fans, food, ushers, etc. It was a great experience.

At one point in the game I was standing next to a KIRO-7 reporter named Deborah Horne. One of the most professional and thorough broadcast journalists in the business, Deborah was also known for being bold and outspoken at times.

There were several controversial calls against the Seahawks that day that probably cost them the game against the Steelers in a 21-10 loss, but the play I remember most was a good one for the Seahawks, if not for me personally.

I was standing next to Deborah Horne when Seahawks left cornerback Kelly Herndon intercepted a Ben Roethlisberger pass and ran it back 76 yards, setting up a Seahawks touchdown that closed the scoring gap to 14-10, Steelers.

As soon as Herndon picked off the pass, Deborah began jumping up and down screaming, "Go Hawks!" in the middle of the press box. There's a hard and fast rule in NFL press boxes and, in fact, in every professional sport that simply states, "No cheering in the press box."

Ejected

As soon as Deborah let loose with her cheer and end zone dance she realized what she'd done and quickly moved to the other side of the room, leaving me standing in direct line with the NFL press box official. "You have to leave now, sir. There's no cheering in the press box; you must leave the stadium." How in the world he mistook Deborah's touchdown celebration for my low key, stone-faced, rule-following self, I'll never know. But I was a goner, ejected from my first Super Bowl for standing too close to someone who had the audacity to cheer in the press box.

As it turned out, I just held back a burst of laughter for as long as I could, moved to the other side of the massive press box and watched the rest of the game there.

That was the last positive moment in the game for the Seahawks. As I mentioned, two controversial calls killed the Seahawks chances and that first franchise Super Bowl experience turned out to be a downer.

Paul Allen

The only thing that stood out about the rest of that day was the postgame party at the team hotel. The Rolling Stones had performed at halftime and Seahawks owner Paul Allen was a big fan of the Stones. I remember saying to Mr. Allen on the field before the game, "You must be thrilled to have the Stones playing today." Without blinking an eye, he said, "Oh, I know those guys well. Yeah, they're great."

As disappointed as Mr. Allen and the staff were in the hotel that night, he did his best to make the best of the weekend by jamming with his guitar and band 'til the wee hours of Monday morning.

High Point

Little did we know at the time but that season would be the high point of
Mike Holmgren's coaching career in Seattle. It's funny when you think about it.
Holmgren could've easily had three Super Bowl championships to his credit as
a head coach.

Many observers feel he was cheated out of a victory that day in Detroit,
and just a year after his Brett Favre team won Super Bowl XXXI, beating the
Patriots 35-21, they led the Denver Broncos most of the way before losing a
heartbreaker, 31-24, in San Diego on January 25, 1998.

Leaving Kirkland

In Holmgren's next three seasons the team finished 9-7, 10-6 and 4-12. I
recall vividly the final home game of the 2008 season on December 21. On the
first official day of winter Seattle was getting belted with an unusual drifting
snowstorm. The Seahawks beat the New York Jets, 13-3, in what was Holmgren's
final victory as coach. He had announced a few days earlier that he would not
be back for another season. Mike Holmgren had brought the thrill of Seahawks
football back to Seattle. His Seahawks record was 86-74. Overall, Holmgren's
teams were 161-111 in his long and distinguished coaching career. There is still
a street named after him in Green Bay.

In the summer before Holmgren's final season the Seahawks moved into a
beautiful new facility on the shores of Lake Washington, on 19 acres owned
by Paul Allen. I remember Mike's first day at the new building, when he noted
candidly that the team didn't really need this big a facility.

Mike was part of the old school of coaches and rapid change was coming
in the NFL. Stadiums once named for the team or a local citizen were all going
corporate. Seahawks Stadium became Qwest Field and later CenturyLink Field.

I don't like the trend, but I understand the business sense of it. I suppose one
day if an old codger with enough money wants a stadium named after him, we'll
be watching games at "Cranky Bob Field," or "Get Off My Lawn Stadium."

Shortly after Holmgren left the team, former Atlanta Falcons coach Jim
Mora was named head coach. Mora had played at the University of Washington

and, in fact, while coaching Atlanta told a radio talk show host that coaching the UW Huskies would be a great job for him. That didn't sit well with the Falcons and soon Mora was on his way to Seattle, not headed for Montlake but the Seahawks.

A Tough Year

I recall early in the summer of 2009, right after Mora got the job, he led a party of climbers up Mount Rainier. The party included NFL Commissioner Roger Goodell and KING-5 sportscaster Paul Silvi. For the record, Silvi had a much easier climb than Goodell, but they both made it back in one piece.

As it turned out that was the highlight of Mora's single season in Seattle. He had great enthusiasm, loved his job, got involved in the community with his wife and family, but he just couldn't get enough momentum to create a winner. The Seahawks finished 5-11 and Mora was fired.

Sounders Return

By now I had become a full-time employee, thanks to Dave Pearson and Bill Chapin who brought me in to help out the newly-formed Seattle Sounders and the Seahawks in digitial media. I had to learn soccer on the fly and enjoyed the process.

I really liked the players and their enthusiasm for the game and the city. Coach Sigi Schmid was patient with me since I didn't know the game, and I always appreciated that. I'll never forget that opening victory over the New York Red Bulls at Qwest Field in 2009. I'd covered the original Sounders when Alan Hinton was coach and was happy for him and all the men and women who worked so hard to bring professional soccer back to Seattle.

Coach Pete

On January 11, 2010, Pete Carroll became head coach of the Seahawks, and nine days later John Schneider was hired as general manager. To borrow a famous phrase from the movie *Casablanca*, "It was the beginning of a beautiful friendship," not to mention the best run of success in Seahawks history.

I will never forget meeting Coach Carroll for our first interview in the Sea Gals dance studio at team headquarters. I had just written a second edition of *Smile in the Mirror*, and handed it to Coach Carroll as he sat down. He smiled and said thanks. I wonder if he ever read it?

The interview went great. I will always remember one thing he said that day when I asked him how he'd had so much success developing players and winners at USC. Carroll said, "As a coach, you need to get to know all of your players, find out what they do best, enhance that part of their game and personality, and then challenge them to do even better."

It's the same philosophy Carroll used to win all those Pac-12 titles, four Rose Bowls, two Orange Bowls and two AP national titles at USC.

He'd been a head coach before in the NFL, one season with the Jets in 1994 and three with the Patriots from 1997-1999.

Me and
Coach Carroll

High Energy

To say that Pete Carroll is a high-energy person and coach is to short-change him in both areas. A lot of people have high energy, but it doesn't always translate into success. In Carroll's case his high energy is part of the process he uses to implement and promote his philosophy. One cannot teach how to "Win Forever" without knowing how to win and knowing how to get others to follow that process.

One might say that Patriots coach Bill Belichick is a proven winner and he's anything but high energy. That's true but there's a key difference between Belichick's way of coaching and Carroll's. In New England, the players follow Belichick because they have to in order to succeed. In Seattle, the players follow Carroll in order to succeed but also because they want to.

Massive Changes

The Seahawks' needs were many that first year, so Carroll and Schneider worked day and night to make whatever moves they could to put a winner on the field as soon as possible, but more importantly create a culture of competition that would permeate the building from locker room to board room.

Among the many early moves, the team acquired running back Marshawn Lynch from the Buffalo Bills on October 5, 2010.

On January 2, 2011 Charlie Whitehurst, playing for the injured Matt Hasselbeck, led the Seahawks over the St. Louis Rams, 16-6. That game clinched Seattle first place in the NFC West and made them the first team in NFL history to make the playoffs with a sub-.500 record of 7-9.

Then on January 8, 2011 seismographs in Seattle would forever become part of sports history. Against the visiting New Orleans Saints, the reigning Super Bowl champions, Marshawn Lynch electrified the crowd at CenturyLink with an amazing, tackle-busting, 67-yard touchdown run that sealed a 41-36 upset playoff victory. The roar of the crowd on that play registered activity on the Pacific Northwest Seismic Network. The play will forever be known as "Beastquake."

Welcome Russell Wilson

Almost daily Schneider and Carroll orchestrated positive changes to the Seahawks roster. On March 20, 2011, they signed upcoming Packers quarterback Matt Flynn to a multiyear contract. Fans assumed that Flynn would be the starter for many seasons to come. Then on April 27, the second day of the NFL Draft, the Seahawks picked quarterback Russell Wilson, 75th overall. Little did anyone know at the time that the move was one of the most important in the history of the franchise. I would be remiss not to mention that Bobby Wagner was also chosen in that draft.

Training Camp

In late July at Seahawks training camp it was expected that Flynn would get most of the snaps in practice and the preseason games. After all, the team had put up fairly big money to get Flynn. After the first two preseason games, Flynn suffered an injury to his throwing arm. That made the decision to start Wilson against the Chiefs at Kansas City a foregone conclusion. The Seahawks won the game, 44-14, and Wilson won the starting job in his rookie year.

Team Travel

Traveling with the team the next few years will always be among my fondest memories. We'd meet the airline security agents at the Seahawks team facility two hours before our chartered flight, get checked-in right there and board a bus for SeaTac Airport.

Each of the staff members had a seat in coach with an empty seat next to it. I chose the aisle seat and used my window seat for my lap top and bag. It gave me plenty of room to work, which after the games was essential.

Our digital media writer Clare Farnsworth sat in front of me with photographer Rod Mar in front of him. Others in the digital media department at the time were Brian Pan, Huy Nguyen and Kenton Olson.

The coaches and executives sat up front in first class with the players using the entire rear section of the plane.

Quiet Flights

People always ask me whether there's a party atmosphere on the plane after a victory or just the opposite after a defeat. Honestly, you can't tell the difference, with just a few exceptions.

I remember coming back the day after beating the Broncos, 43-8, for the Super Bowl title in New Jersey. It was snowing hard as we left the hotel in Jersey City for Newark airport. We barely got off the ground before the other four Seahawks staff and fan planes were delayed.

As I got onto the plane I saw Coach Carroll sitting next to John Schneider up front. Schneider smiled at coach and said casually, "By the way, Pete, we won." Everybody laughed. That was about the last sound I heard for the next couple of hours. Most of the players were sleeping as were the staff members, with the exception of the team video crew, photographers Corky Trewin and Mar and a few others.

Suddenly, about an hour out from Seattle, soft-spoken kicker Steven Hauschka came through the cabin yelling, "Hey, what's the matter with everyone? We just

Tyler Lockett 2015

won the Super Bowl!" There was little response. The players kept sleeping and Hauschka went back to his seat.

Visiting Cities

I must admit I enjoyed Saturdays in visiting cities almost as much as game days. Being a big fan of "live" theater, I took advantage of some terrific shows in my 11 years on the road with the Seahawks.

In New York I saw the Tony Award-winning show *Jersey Boys* in 2007, and in later years shows like *Chicago* and *The Producers*. On a wintry afternoon in Chicago one December I got the last available seat to see the wonderful musical, *A Christmas Story*.

As a member of the staff I often took advantage of the team meals in visiting hotels. An entire ballroom would be dedicated to the team meal on Saturday night and again on Sunday mornings before the game.

I enjoyed going to "chapel" at the hotels on Saturday nights. Usually one of the players would connect with a chaplain in the city the team would visit, and that person would stop by Saturday night at the hotel to do a short service for anyone interested in attending.

With Lombardi Trophy 2014

Game Day

Game Day always started off quietly. The players would board three buses to the stadium with staff on another bus. We'd usually arrive two hours before game time, set-up the postgame press conference room and get situated in the press box.

I would always scout out the visiting players locker room since they were often smaller than the home locker rooms. That way I have an advanced look at how close the lockers were to each other. Often, after a game, win or lose, it was a challenge maneuvering around wet towels piled on the floor, reporters crowding around players' lockers with coaches crisscrossing through the room to and from the showers.

In this case it was much better after a win than a loss. There was a notable difference. After a win on the road the wet towels, silly questions from network reporters and players trying to answer them while dressing didn't seem so annoying. After a loss, it was significantly more quiet in the locker room, almost as if we were walking in a cemetery at night, not wanting something bad to happen.

Having said that, though, I never had a negative incident with a player or coach after a game. I always figured it would be easier to get a response from a player whose team just lost a game by having a conversation with him, not an interrogation of him.

Shock in Arizona

After flying so high in New Jersey with a win over the Broncos, the 2014 Seahawks made it back to the Super Bowl with an unlikely comeback win over the Packers in the NFC title game.

Now that I've set this up, you're already re-playing the Malcolm Butler interception of a Russell Wilson pass on the one-yard-line, the most heartbreaking single moment in Seattle sports history. Some say the team still is carrying the pain of that loss. I don't agree with that, but let's not be naïve; it hurt like heck at the time and for weeks afterwards.

Postgame

I will never forget two things from the hour immediately following that game. I was on my way to the winners' postgame staging area when the play happened. I watched it on a small monitor near the ceiling of one of the tunnels leaving the field. Instead of going left into the winners' interview zone, I turned right to find the other postgame room. Believe me, the difference is like night and day. From a brightly lit room with banners and balloons and music to a darker, much quieter and smaller area, still large enough for the network and a few local cameras to record heartache live around the world.

Once the interception happened it was over, but with the emotion on the field delaying the inevitable, it seemed like an hour before I saw Coach Carroll enter the room. He walked in behind me, patted me on the shoulder and said, "How you doing, Tony?"

Amazing. This man, whose team just lost a heartbreaker on a last-second play, took the time to ask me how I was doing.

Coach Carroll answered all the questions the press peppered him with for 25 minutes and then, one by one, some of the players came through to do the same. I really don't remember much of the rest of that night. All I wanted to do was get home and move on. Easy for me to say. I'm not a player. But I felt for the players and coaches because I'd been with them every step of the way. I would be fine in a day or so, but I sensed that it would take them much longer.

Next Morning

I mentioned the team meals earlier in this chapter. In this case, since we stayed over Sunday in Arizona, there was a team breakfast provided the next day, Monday morning, from 8-11 a.m. I wandered into an empty meal room at 8:15, not a single player or coach to be seen. I walked over to the food line and grabbed a few pieces of fresh fruit. As I turned to my left Russell Wilson was standing there. He looked at me and said, "How's it going, Tony? Tough one yesterday, huh?" What could I say except, "Yeah, tough one, but you guys will bounce back. You always do." He nodded and walked away.

In the course of a few hours I'd come face to face with two of the people most affected by that disappointing loss, and both asked me how I was doing. That should explain why I have so much admiration for Pete Carroll, Russell Wilson and the Seahawks organization. It is a family, and I'm so grateful I had a chance to be part of that family for 11 years.

A Reason to Smile

I met a lot of really good people when I covered the Seahawks for 22 years and later worked for the team. In 1981, when I first arrived in Seattle, I asked Jim Zorn to sign a photo so I could send it to my friend Rick, the 12-year-old who was fighting cancer back in Indiana. Jim did much better than that. He called Rick and spent 20 minutes on the phone with words of encouragement and even a prayer. I'll always be grateful for that.

Through the years there were so many others whose friendship I valued, including Paul Johns, who was forced to retire because of a neck injury early in his career and spent a season as my co-host on the KING-5 Seahawks postgame

show. Sam Adkins worked the same show with me at KIRO-7 a few years later and became a good friend too, as did Dave Wyman, who has continued his radio career on 710 ESPN Seattle.

I never gave much of an effort to be friends with the active players. I figured they had their own friends and chose to keep a professional distance, but there

With Doug Baldwin in Yakima

were a couple of guys I got close to and I'm grateful for that. One was receiver Bobby Engram, who came to me and asked for advice with public speaking. Left tackle Russell Okung was a good friend. I'll never forget his first season as a rookie. He found out I was doing a lot of work in the community and asked for ways to become involved.

Doug Baldwin and I traveled to Yakima in 2014 to speak at a YMCA fundraiser. We spent 40 minutes on stage in a talk show format, and then Doug spent another hour taking photos and signing autographs for fans. All of those relationships and memories make me smile.

CHAPTER TEN

Baseball Leads Again

"The one constant through all the years has been baseball."

– James Earl Jones

Pardon the pun here but it seems to me that baseball has always been a little ahead of the curve when it comes to social reform.

During World War II baseball followed the lead of the rest of America, sending some of its biggest stars into the various armed services and in some cases into combat. The list is long and impressive. Ted Williams was a willing fighter pilot, Yogi Berra volunteered to be part of the invasion of Normandy, Hank Greenberg, Joe Dimaggio, Stan Musial and dozens of others volunteered to serve their country.

A few years later in the spring of 1947 baseball led the way for America when Jackie Robinson became the first black player in the major leagues, thanks to a partnership with Brooklyn Dodgers' General Manager Branch Rickey. It took the country 17 more years to enact Civil Rights legislation under the Lyndon Johnson presidency.

Fast forward to 2017 and the World Baseball Championships. Big league players from every team in both leagues are playing for their home countries in this most patriotic tribute to what was once called "The National Pastime." Baseball may not be first in the hearts of Americans anymore with the growth of the National Football League, but it still leads the way as far as social awareness is concerned.

While many in our country including our new president preach daily about "America First," and spread the fears of globalization, baseball leads by example.

Players like Mariners pitcher Felix Hernandez who'll pitch for Venezuela and Seattle Mariner teammates Robinson Cano, Nelson Cruz and Jean Segura who'll play for the Dominican Republic can still love America while playing baseball for their countries of origin for two weeks.

Baseball is the best example of what mankind can be if you really think about it. In baseball once a man is on first base, a teammate may be asked by his coach to "sacrifice bunt," allowing the runner to advance to second base. Who can imagine giving up their own freedom or in this case "at bat" to allow a teammate to succeed? That's what you do in baseball. If we did more of this in America we truly would be "great again."

So while some in this country and many around the world are rejecting what is called globalization for what is called nationalism I'm suggesting that we embrace both. Why can't one be proud of his own country while still respecting the rest of the world? That leads to peace, which I'm sure to many is a sign of weakness.

The alternative is to spread fear and hatred from our borders outward, building walls real and imagined between us and the rest of the world. That leads to mistrust, ignorance, fear and a false sense of pride and all that leads to war. Do we really want more war? Have we not learned anything from history?

Time to look at baseball as the leader it is. Time to see it as a glowing example of what's right in America. Any activity that calls for all participants to work for and with one another towards a common goal is an activity worth cheering for.

Baseball is ahead of the curve which seems rather poetic since one who can't catch up to a curve will not succeed in baseball or in life.

CHAPTER ELEVEN

Home Run Summer

"There it is, there it is, if it stays fair there it is, number 60."
– Mel Allen 1961

In the summer of 1961 the New York Yankees were again surging to the top of the American League standings. The big story in sports that year was the historic home run battle between teammates Mickey Mantle and Roger Maris.

Mantle was the Yankees golden boy, a combination of muscle and country boy good looks out of Commerce, Oklahoma. The soft-spoken Yankees center fielder had won the Triple Crown in 1956 and annually grabbed the headlines in the *New York Daily News* and *New York Times*.

At the end of the 1959 season the Yankees traded for outfielder Roger Maris. He was a brilliant defensive player with a rocket arm and a flawless left-handed swing. Maris hit 39 homers in his first Yankee season. In 1961 he would battle Mantle day after day for the major league lead.

Only when the oft-injured Mantle got hurt again in September did Maris surge ahead in the race. The press and the fans favored Mantle as the M & M boys raced towards Babe Ruth's single season record. Maris began to lose chucks of hair because of the pressure and later near the end of his life told a friend, "I wish I'd never hit all those home runs."

On the final day of the regular season Maris hit a fastball off Red Sox starter Tracy Stallard into the short right field seats for number 61. He couldn't even enjoy the feat since the American League decided to place an asterisk next to the record since his 61 homers came in 162 games and not 154 during Ruth's record season of 1927. Mantle finished his shortened season with 54 home runs and remained a Yankee till his career ended in 1968. Maris was traded to the St. Louis Cardinals after the 1964 season.

CHAPTER TWELVE

Love for Theater

"Movies will make you famous; television will make you rich;
but theater will make you good."

– Terrence Mann

L ast summer I played two different characters in the Woodinville Rep's production of *Plaza Suite*. It was my sixth decade in community theater. For as long as I can remember, I've been fascinated by "live" theater. I grew up in Wilton, Connecticut, home of the Wilton Playshop.

Established in 1937 and located at 15 Lovers Lane, the classic barn-style building has been home to some of the best theater in the country. I saw my first show there in the late 60s, a wonderful production of *Barefoot in the Park*.

Like so many community theaters across the country, Wilton Playshop has a full schedule of stage productions throughout the calendar year.

A few miles away is the famous Westport Country Playhouse, a summer stock theater that often features some of the best-known Broadway performers.

First Show

After working on the Senior Show in high school as a writer and master of ceremonies, I was curious about local theater. It's one thing to host a talent show and ad-lib most of your lines, but auditioning for a part, learning lines and a character and rehearsing for six weeks is a whole different story.

I heard about a local theater in Redding called the Bonner Playhouse. They were doing a production of *What a Life* and needed young male actors for the lead and backup roles.

The director was a man named W. Thomas Littleton, the first gay man I ever met. This was the late 60s when being gay was not something one discussed much, yet in the theater community was taken in stride by everyone.

I read a few lines for one of the characters and did not impress. As I sat watching the other actors I figured my theater career would begin and end on the same night. After about an hour, our exasperated director had still not found his lead actor to play a character named Henry Aldrich.

Last Resort

Suddenly he looked at me and said, "Tony, come on up here and read for Henry." By that time, I had nothing to lose and over-played my audition just for the fun of it. "That's it, you're Henry," shouted Littleton. "Much better read this time." Thus began my community theater career.

On opening night, the Bonner Playhouse was packed. My mother had talked my father into coming to the show. Actually he was curious about my skills on stage after seeing my performance in the Wilton High School Senior Show six years earlier, though he would rather be fishing than sitting in a stuffy old building for two hours. Opening night went great, though, and Dad said he liked the show.

Second Night Blues

As we scurried around the dressing room after opening night I'll never forget what our director said. "Good job everyone, but don't let this go to your head. Don't have a second night letdown."

I thought he was just being a downer, so I ignored him. I'll never make that mistake again.

On the second night of the show nine people sat in the audience when the curtain opened. Thank goodness my mother was one of them, otherwise no one would have been laughing. My performance was flat, the show was flat and our director just looked at us afterwards and said, "OK, let it go. We'll be fine for the rest of the run." He didn't need to say, "I told you so"; we proved it to ourselves.

Whether it's a play or a baseball game, I learned to never be satisfied with my performance. Celebrate it, learn from it and then let it go and make the next show or game even better.

I did a few more shows at the Bonner Playhouse, including Neil Simon's *Odd Couple* in the early 70s. I played the taxi driver named "Speed." I had a blast, but that ended my stage career for almost 20 years. My work and family didn't allow much time for learning lines or rehearsing.

In the early 80s I moved to Seattle for a job in television. I had continued to support community theater since my stage debut years earlier, but only as an audience member. I'd seen *Grease* on Broadway and countless shows in local theaters everywhere I lived, but I never gave much thought to acting again.

That changed one spring evening in 1986 when I got a call from a group called the Lighthouse Theater in Mukilteo, Washington. "We were wondering if you and your news anchor Aaron Brown would be interested in playing Oscar and Felix in our production of *The Odd Couple*." I was flattered by the offer. Aaron laughed and quickly said, "No thanks, you do it."

As it turned out the plans changed when Lighthouse couldn't get the rights for the show that summer and decided instead to do *A Thousand Clowns*.

So began my second career in community theater, as Murray Burns, hard-partying, carefree mentor, and father figure for his 12-year-old nephew. I had to learn about 75 pages of lines and sing a song for the show, but it was one of the most rewarding experiences of my life.

Another rewarding experience was the review I received from the *Everett Herald*. "Sportscaster recites lines like he's reading the baseball scores," screamed the headline on the day after opening night. My colleagues didn't say a word as we dressed for the Saturday performance until finally our director, a woman named Feather, told me to ignore the local critics. "That critic is always harsh. She doesn't know what she's doing," Feather told me. That opened the floodgates for the actors and crew to further coddle me with similar comments.

Lesson Learned

I listened politely and then said, "Look, the critic has seen hundreds of shows. She must have an idea of what's good and bad and in between. I'm going to call her and ask her what she saw and how I can improve." The following Monday morning I called the *Herald* and got the critic on the phone. She may have expected a complaint but that wasn't my goal. "What can I do to improve?" I asked her. She was surprised, to say the least. "Honestly, Tony, I've never had an actor ask me that without first complaining about the review. My advice is to slow down, feel the lines, don't rush, and you'll be fine."

The next Friday evening I did exactly that. It was my first real acting lesson and it came from a theater critic.

Rosehill Players

A month or so after the four-weekend run of *A Thousand Clowns*, I got a call from the Rosehill Community Center, formerly the Rosehill elementary school and our show venue. "Mr. Ventrella, we're wondering if someone is going to pay the bill for the custodian and rental on the last show. Apparently Lighthouse Theater has gone out of business and they still owe us money."

That marked the beginning of a long and wonderful run as co-founder of the Rosehill Players with longtime friend David Blacker. We paid off the debt and came right back the following summer with a production of *The Odd Couple* with me as Oscar Madison, Gregg Hays as Felix Unger and David as Murray the Cop. We had a blast and ran with it from there, producing shows every summer for the next 14 years.

Dave and Gregg
backstage *Chapter Two*

Chapter Two

David, Gregg and I met early in 1988 and decided to make *Chapter Two* our inaugural Rosehill Players show. Open auditions began in early April for a show that needed only four actors, two men and two women. Gregg would direct, David and I would play the male leads, George Schneider and his brother Leo. We needed two females, one to play the lead character Jennie and one for her best friend Faye. We decided on a local actress named Gretchen for the part of Faye. She'd already starred in *The Odd Couple* as one of the Pigeon sisters and brought a solid acting background with her to the stage for *Chapter Two*. The search began for a co-lead, a woman who could play the love interest to George, a demanding and dramatic role for community theater.

Chapter Two, written by Neil Simon, was really the story of his second marriage and the struggles of two individuals on the rebound, one from a divorce and the other a widower deeply in love with his first wife.

After two nights of auditioning several women for the part, Gregg was undecided and felt he needed more time. Then suddenly out of the blue came a young lady named Dottie who had just moved to the area from New York City, where she'd spent a year working on Wall Street. She was living in Mukilteo and working at a local restaurant while pondering the rest of her life and career. Dottie was 24 years old and a graduate of M.I.T. with a major in business but a love for theater.

Dottie's Audition

It was a Monday evening when David and Gregg brought Dottie in to read with me at KING-5 TV. She was a very attractive brunette, not lacking in confidence or conversational skills. The audition went great and Dottie was cast as Jennie.

Theater Romance

I am certain that in community theaters across the world actors have met and fallen in love with other actors millions of times. When you work closely together in a play, especially the male and female lead for six to eight weeks, then perform for another month, things sometimes happen.

It happened with Dottie and me. I left my girlfriend, Dottie left her boyfriend, we did the show and had a summer romance.

As we got to know each other it became clear to me that Dottie's goals and dreams had nothing to do with Wall Street or the Mukilteo restaurant she worked at. In one of our many late night chats on the Mukilteo beach she told me about her dream to become a writer, a famous writer.

Go for It

Funny thing about summer romances, especially those that start in the theater. They tend to cool down when the reality of life sets in. I could hear the passion in Dottie's voice when she talked about becoming a writer. I also knew that to realize that passion she would have to move away, which would put a major damper on our future. I encouraged her to go.

U.C. Davis

Dottie applied and easily got into the master's writing program at U.C. Davis. She would leave in late August. In fact, she and I drove her 12-year-old Ford Torino from Mukilteo to Davis, California one weekend so she could start her new life.

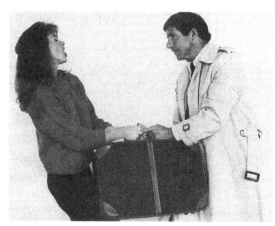

Dottie & Me in
Chapter Two

We stayed in touch daily that school year, and I made several weekend trips to California to see her. We were slowly drifting apart but still close enough to keep the fire burning a few more months.

When Dottie came home for Christmas in December we both had a decision to make. Would we continue a long-distance relationship or part friends and reach for our separate goals? It's a story that plays itself out thousands of times every day. It's the basis for so many movies, whether it's *The Notebook* or *La La Land*, take your pick, the story is as old as love itself.

Dottie had shown me her late grandmother's wedding ring the summer before, so I thought it would be nice to have it restored and cleaned and give it back to her at Christmas.

It turned out to be an awkward yet revealing moment in our lives. On Christmas morning I presented this beautiful box to Dottie. She opened it and was thrilled to see the ring, completely restored and fitted to her finger. I will never forget what happened next. She put the ring on her finger, looked into my eyes and we said simultaneously, "Now what do we do?" We both laughed, realizing that although we still cared deeply for each other, there would be no wedding, no marriage to each other but with any luck a lasting friendship.

Fame and Fortune

We kept in touch after that Christmas, but for the most part the romance that began as George and Jennie on a Mukilteo stage in *Chapter Two* would fade into history like the lines we knew so well in the summer of 1988.

One day in the early spring Dottie called to tell me she'd sold her first script to a TV show called *China Beach*, and a few months later, a second script. She was on her way to a new career.

In the next few years I heard progress reports from Dottie through David Blacker and occasionally from Dottie herself. Then in the summer of 1998 Dottie called with an invitation to lunch. She was coming back to Mukilteo for a wedding.

Back on Stage

We met in front of the Rosehill Community Center on a summer afternoon and talked for an hour while sitting on the sidewalk. Then we went inside and had our picture taken on the old stage. It had been ten years since our time together in *Chapter Two*.

At lunch later in the day I told Dottie I'd pick up the tab and she said, "No, I've got this one. I've had a good year."

I was aware that she was a big part of the hit television show, *Caroline in the City*, based in part on her own life in New York during her Wall Street years, but I had no idea of the success she was having with her current show, *Dharma and Greg*.

I remember saying, "So Dottie, how's it going?" She laughed and said, "This is crazy, Tony. Would you believe I made 21 million dollars last year?" Without missing a beat, I said, "Not only do I believe it, but you're paying for lunch." We had a great laugh over it, spent the next hour talking about our lives since 1988 and then said goodbye.

A year or so later Dottie invited my son Peter to Los Angeles and took him on a tour of the *Dharma and Greg* set. The last I heard, Dottie was living in the Malibu area with her family. I think of her every time I perform in community theater. She was certainly the greatest success story to come out of community theater that I knew, but there were so many more, at different levels that never got written or talked about.

Irene Griffore

There was our prop mistress, Irene Griffore, a British war bride who survived the Nazi Blitzkrieg in London and later moved to the Pacific Northwest with her husband. Anytime I had a question about the set or a prop, Irene would say, "The difficult can be done immediately; the impossible will take a little longer."

Billie

Billie was a middle-aged school bus driver whose confidence level was so low she had difficulty facing her own children. David urged her to audition for a show called *Fools*. She won a lead role and later told us, "That play changed my life. I'm so much more confident now. I love to make people laugh."

Talented film and stage actor Marni King took a role in *George Washington Slept Here*, began a relationship with co-star David Dilgard and then married him.

One day a ten-year-old named Jake Ehrler asked if he could be a volunteer at Rosehill. He was a tireless helper, and later took a part in *The Nerd* and even directed one of our shows. Jake passed away a couple of years ago but left a lasting impression on everyone who knew him.

Evergreen Family Theater

I was working for the Seahawks in the spring of 2008 when I got a call from my friend Marsha Stueckle. "I'm starting a theater group inside a church in Redmond. We're opening with *The Diary of Anne Frank*. Would you like to audition?"

Billie and Me
in *Fools*

It had been eight years since my last show in Mukilteo, so of course I said, "Yeah, that sounds like a challenge. I'll do it."

I ended up playing Otto Frank in the Evergreen Family Theater production that spring, along with a cast of talented actors which included a young lady named Olivia playing Anne. She and the rest of that cast gave me something to shoot for every night.

Marsha, our founder and director, is one of those giving souls who exudes love, kindness and a lightning-fast sense of humor. For nearly ten years Marsha and her team of friends and cohorts, led by Michelle and Karen, put on some of the best community theater this area has ever seen. Every summer the church was abuzz with kids' camps, singing and dancing and a little praying as well.

In 2014 I was proud to be part of a two-person production of *Tuesdays with Morrie* with Huy Nguyen. We did a benefit performance for the local chapter of ALS, raising $3000 for research. Several members of our audience were challenged with ALS which brought me a deep appreciation of what they're going through and how much they care for others.

Thanks to Marsha for allowing me to be a part of the Evergreen Family Theater all those years and for introducing my grandchildren Preston, Edie and Emmett to the theater scene.

As I write this, Preston and Edie are attending Woodinville High School and are thrilled to be involved in that wonderful theater program.

The Diary of Anne Frank – 2008

Thanks also to Hjalmer Anderson, longtime director of theater at Woodinville for keeping Woodinville Rep going strong and for allowing me to play two roles in *Plaza Suite* in 2016.

Value or Theater

So many lives are transformed by community and school theater. That's why it is a crime that our federal and state governments do so little to support the arts. Not every child can play football or baseball, but all of them can be part of a show, whether it's backstage making the set come to life or on-stage making a character come to life.

My grandniece Nina will earn a Bachelor of Fine Arts and Musical Theater degree from the University of Hartford Hartt School in 2018. She calls theater training a "safe space to make bold decisions. It's been proven over and over again that young people who receive drama and theater training in their early years show improved growth in self-esteem and emotional stability." Nina adds, "and those skills can be transformed into other classes and real-life situations."

Our Director
Marsha

A Reason to Smile

I've joined a couple of friends who love theater and together we're trying to launch a small community group in my hometown. I'm confident we can make people laugh, cry, maybe even applaud in the coming years.

CHAPTER THIRTEEN

Every 15 Minutes

"Do what you need to do, when you need to do it,
whether you like it or not."

– Gordon Thomas

In October of 2017 the Wilton High School Class of 1962 will gather for its 55th reunion. How in the world did that happen? Where did the time go? What happened to all of us? Wasn't it yesterday we sat in the combination auditorium-gym-cafeteria at Wilton High School and listened to our principal, Gordon Thomas, deliver the commencement address? Here's what's wild, I actually remember one thing he said. In fact, I'll never forget it.

"I want to leave here today with one bit of advice that will help you through your entire lives," Mr. Thomas said. "Do what you need to do, when you need to do it, whether you like it or not." That was it. It was over. At which point my mother stated really loud so all could hear, "Thank God." Apparently it wasn't a sure bet that I would graduate from high school, but it happened on that day in 1962, yes, 55 years ago.

Wilton High School, as I knew it, was actually a combination junior-senior high school. The town was building a new high school, set to open in the fall of 1962, just two months after my graduation.

I was obviously a big sports fan, but I also loved theater and was, in fact, one of the producers of the Senior Show in spring of 1962. Working with classmates Liz Ward and Martha Ingerson, along with many others, we wrote an original sitcom script about our school. We called it *Educapers*, and to this day it is still the only originally scripted senior show in the 58-year history of Wilton High School.

Almost everyone in the Class of '62 had something to do with the show. We did takeoffs on our principal and most of our teachers, and the audience of nearly 1,000 loved it. It is no exaggeration to say that every teacher we spoofed in that show enjoyed the attention. It's also true that since our first reunion in 1972, one of the big topics of discussion is that Senior Show of '62.

I vividly recall joining the entire cast on stage as Lucy Campbell sang *The Party's Over* to her classmates and the audience. The term bittersweet was created for moments like that. We all enjoyed the high of a terrific performance and almost immediately realized that it also signaled the end of our high school years.

Next Step

I still have all four yearbooks from Wilton High School. By my senior year in the fall of 1961 about a quarter of our class had been together since third grade and at least half since freshman year.

Our senior year was busy from the first day. I was involved in planning the Senior Show while most of my classmates were applying or already preparing for college. An astounding 90 percent of my high school class continued their education in either a two- or four-year college. My plan was stay at home, work in my dad's barber shop and attend Wright Technical School in Stamford. "I want you to learn a second trade," Dad told me. "That way you'll always be able to get a job. So off I went to Wright Tech to learn how to become an electrician, not exactly in line with my early childhood dream of being the New York Yankees' play-by-play broadcaster.

I'll never forget the final week of classes in my senior year. That's really when I learned the definition of bittersweet. All of us seemed so close back then, brought together by our day-to-day interaction, year after year, teacher after teacher, class after class.

Betsy Evans

I'm sure the Senior Show was the one single event that made us a family for life. On graduation night, none of us knew what that life would bring or how fragile it would be in the months and years ahead.

Betsy Evans was one of the most popular girls in our class. She was kind, extremely smart and very attractive. The other day I read her message in my yearbook, and it reinforced everything I've just said. I really didn't know Betsy that well and would never get the chance to know her.

After high school Betsy went off to college at Wellesley. Not long into her freshman year she was not feeling well and went in for a checkup. She was diagnosed with leukemia. In December of 1962 I saw her at a Wilton basketball game and said hello. She passed away not long after that. "Betsy was such a rare person with a beautiful heart," close friend Bob Cunningham told me recently. "I remember seeing her when she was home from the hospital resting. A group of us sat around listening to Bob Newhart's new comedy album. We laughed for an hour together." Betsy died shortly after one of those visits. Classmates Paul Heinrich, Nick Homer, Bob Cunningham and others carried her casket. I'll never forget her funeral service at the big Episcopal Church on Route 7 in Wilton. Just months removed from high school we were already saying goodbye to a beloved classmate.

Johnny Corr

Just a few years later, in December of 1967, many of us gathered at the Congregational Church in Wilton for the wedding of Karen Redfern and Bob Serenbetz. Little did we know, another popular and beloved classmate, Johnny Corr, was killed in Viet Nam that same week. Communications were a lot slower in those days. Not even his family knew of his death until several days after it happened. A few weeks later we gathered again to say goodbye to a special friend, one I had known since fourth grade.

First Reunion

Later, in 1971, I got a call from Diane Russell, one of my favorite WHS friends. She and I had won the dubious honor of being "Class Wits" in our yearbook. "We're having a ten-year reunion in Ridgefield," she told me. "Would you come and be our master of ceremonies?" Of course the answer was yes, and why not? I was a ham who thrived on attention and was thrilled to return to the stage ten years after *Educapers*.

Most people will admit that their first high reunion is the most awkward of all. Let's face it, you've only been out of high school ten years. Some classmates already have good jobs, some don't. Some are married, some not. A few look great, some look less great. All in all, though, we had a good time catching up.

1982

I've heard from quite a few friends who attended their 10th reunion and never went to another one. In some cases there never was another to attend. The Wilton High School Class of 1962 was the exception to that rule. In 1982, we met for our 20th reunion. I remember welcoming everyone to the event and jokingly suggesting that we meet every five years after that since we were all at the ripe old age of 38. Apparently the planning committee thought it was a good idea, and there we were five years later for the 25th WHS reunion.

I reached back into my Neil Simon book of one-liners and came up with a new one at the 1987 meeting. "Classmates, we met after ten years, then after 20 and now five years later at 25. After looking at a few of you closely I've concluded that it would be a good idea to meet every 15 minutes from now on; you just never know what's gonna happen." It got a laugh, but deep down inside everyone knew what I was talking about. It felt so good to be together again, but the weekend flew by and we really weren't sure if we'd ever see each other again.

As I write this chapter, that was 30 years ago. We have since had five more reunions, all well attended by most of our classmates and a treasured small group of our teachers like Paula Rutkowsky and Nick Zeoli, and Louise Mariani, our class advisor. Mr. Z, as we all know him, was the highlight of all of our reunions with his high-energy stories and praise for our class as "my favorite class of all at WHS." At our 40th reunion in 2002, Mr. Z did a cartwheel across the floor when I introduced him. He was 78 years old at the time. I got a Christmas card from him last year. He mentioned he walks a mile a day and played 92 holes of golf near his home in Vermont last summer. He is now 93 years old.

I am grateful for another opportunity to gather again in the fall of 2017, to walk the grounds of Wilton High School one more time, to see the faces and hear the voices of old and dear friends. We meet every five years now, but I'm seriously considering mentioning my idea from 2002. Maybe it really is time to plan these WHS reunions every 15 minutes.

A Reason to Smile

I just looked at my high school yearbook and realized that I once wore a skirt to a faculty versus the girls' basketball game. The boys were the cheerleaders. I was Max Klinger before he was.

CHAPTER FOURTEEN

Thank God for Teachers

"If you're planning for a year, plant rice.
If you're planning for a decade, plant trees.
If you're planning for a lifetime, educate people."

– Chinese Proverb

In all of our lives there are at least a few teachers we'll never forget. Dedicated men and women whose passion for sharing their knowledge touched our lives and created a ripple effect that will last forever.

Between elementary, middle school, high school and college it should be easy to pinpoint five teachers who had the most impact on our lives. I'm listing my favorites in chronological order.

Miss Hoag

Her name was Gladys Hoag. Gladys. Now that's a name you don't hear anymore, but it's one I'll never forget. Miss Hoag was my fifth-grade teacher at Center School in Wilton. The year was 1955. Dwight Eisenhower was President, Richard Nixon Vice President. *The Ed Sullivan Show* dominated Sunday night television with guests like Walt Disney, Irving Berlin and Fred Astaire. Sullivan himself was anything but a matinee idol. Rather plain-looking and never totally comfortable on camera, Sullivan nonetheless held his spot on CBS for 23 years.

A typical Sunday night might feature a comedian like Bob Hope, an aria performed by an opera diva, someone spinning dinner plates on wooden dowels, and perhaps a plug for a new movie.

By the way, Sullivan is generally associated with the debut of a handsome rock-and-roll singer from Memphis named Elvis Presley, but that is not exactly how it happened. In fact, Sullivan didn't like Elvis' music and vowed never to invite him on the show. Funny how ego and money tend to drive business decisions though.

Presley's first television appearance was on a little-remembered program called *Stage Show*, co-hosted by Tommy and Jimmy Dorsey. Elvis made six appearances on that show before he was signed by the *Milton Berle Show*, appearing there on April 3, 1956.

Once Sullivan saw his own show getting crushed in the ratings, he changed his tune. Even then Presley appeared on the *Steve Allen Show* before Sullivan could get him on CBS.

Finally, when Elvis did appear on the Sullivan show it attracted an incredible 82.6 percent of the viewing audience.

Center School

I had moved to Wilton with my family in the summer of 1953, attending 3rd grade at Center School. However, the following year, with the school undergoing a major renovation, all 4th graders were bused to the local Congregational Church. It was crowded and the playground was small, so when we moved back to Center School in the fall of 1954 it was almost like being in a new school.

Miss Hoag's class was on the southeast corner of the school, just across the access road from the Angelique perfume factory. I only mention this because my mom, who was one of the first working mothers I knew, worked at that factory. She was literally two minutes away from me at all times. There is no way I could've gotten into trouble and not had my mother know about it.

The good news is no one got into trouble in Miss Hoag's class. It wasn't because she was easy on us. On the contrary, she was a retired U.S. Army sergeant and didn't take any nonsense from anyone. But she was also fair and a lot of fun, and as a bonus she was a heck of a softball player, which made our class very competitive in playground softball games.

Popsicles for Everyone

One memorable day in Miss Hoag's class came in mid-June, near the end of the school year. The weather had turned hot early that year, so one day Miss Hoag sent a few of us across the street to the Village Market for Popsicles. She bought the entire class Popsicles. Sometimes in life, just when you're convinced you've got it made, something happens to bring you back to reality.

Just as we were opening our Popsicles and taking that first cool, tasty bite, the door to the classroom opened and in stepped our principal. In a flash Miss Hoag greeted her boss while signaling behind her back for us to hide the Popsicles in our desks. Thinking fast and talking just as fast, Miss Hoag quickly escorted the principal into the hall, explaining that she had just called a pop quiz on us and didn't want to lose the momentum or the surprise.

I will never forget the smile on her face when she came back into the classroom a few minutes later and said, "Okay, take them out and finish them up." We quickly shoved the half-melted Popsicles in our mouths and gained even more love and respect for our 5th grade teacher.

Hans Collischonn

We were all afraid of him at first. He was a towering figure who seemed much taller than 6'2" because of his long, purposeful strides and enormous feet, always decked out in perfectly shined black shoes. He spoke with a loud, booming, confident voice, almost as if he was commanding a platoon of soldiers. It didn't take long for us to learn that a good portion of his life was spent as an officer in the Army. When I had Mr. Collischonn for social studies in 7th grade he was a major in the Army Reserves. He never addressed his students by their first names; it was always Mr. Ventrella, Mr. Heinrich or Miss Grimm, Miss Thompson. He was respectful of every student. Not once in all the years I knew Mr. Collischonn did I hear him put down a student in front of other students.

I admit that the first few days in Mr. Collischonn's class at Wilton Junior-Senior High School were a little stressful, but then all of a sudden one day I realized I wasn't intimidated anymore. The reason was simple, Mr. Collischonn was a great teacher.

He didn't just cover people, events and dates in history, he brought them to life with an enthusiasm for storytelling and a flair for theatrics that kept his students engaged from start to finish of every class. He was Mark Twain and John Wayne all rolled into one.

I can't recall most of the lessons in social studies from my 7th grade teacher, but I will never forget a story he told us in the days leading up to Christmas that year.

Mr. Collischonn was born to German immigrants and lived in Connecticut just a few miles north of our high school. Each Christmas his father cut down an evergreen tree from the family property and put it up in the living room with lights, tinsel and colorful homemade decorations. Now, when I say lights I'm not talking about electric lights, I'm talking real candles with real flames. That's right, an old German tradition was played out every year in the Collischonn household during my teacher's childhood.

Just about the time Mr. C was a young teen, electric Christmas lights became available, but you'd never find them on the Collischonn family tree. "My father didn't trust electricity enough to drape wires and lights on a tree inside the house. He was afraid something would go wrong and there would be a fire. So even though real flames from real candles seemed dangerous, we stuck with them for most of my childhood," Mr. Collischonn explained.

Finally, the year Mr. Collischonn turned 16 his father gave in and bought a string of electric lights for the tree—and on the second night a spark from one of the wires set the tree on fire. As Mr. C explained the story in detail we all sat there wide-eyed, picturing a ball of flame lighting up Christmas many years ago. Mr. Collischoon assured us that no one was hurt and the damage was minimal, but from that year on, for the rest of his father's life, the Collischonn Christmas tree had real candles with real flames.

I didn't have Mr. C for any classes in high school, but since our little town had a combined junior high and high school I did see him occasionally in the hallways. After I graduated I went to a vocational school for a year before joining the Army. Keep in mind that in 1964 the Viet Nam war was beginning to escalate. It seemed like President Johnson was sending more troops to Southeast Asia every time he opened his mouth.

Recruiting Office

On a Friday afternoon in Stamford, Conn., after attending classes at Wright Technical School, I stopped by an Army recruiting office to sign up. It was 5 o'clock. The recruiting sergeant was cordial and welcoming but asked me to come back on Monday since he was too busy with paperwork.

By Monday I'd decided to join the Army Reserves instead and signed up at the 318th Signal Corps in Danbury, Conn. I would begin my Reserves meetings the following month and ship off to active duty in the spring.

Major Collischonn

I got a short haircut at my dad's barber shop the next day and attended my first meeting at the Army Reserve Center the following week. As I stood in line with the other recruits waiting for my first meeting, I heard a familiar voice say, "Mr. Ventrella, we meet again." Sure enough, there stood the towering figure, wearing a crewcut and combat boots, his voice booming gloriously. It was my 7th grade social studies teacher, Hans Collischonn. He was in full fatigue uniform with gold, major clusters on each side of his collar. Mr. C from Wilton Junior High was now Major Collischonn of the 318th Signal Corps. As intimidated as I was in Mr. C's presence as a 7th grader, I was happy to see a familiar face on my first day in the Army.

For the next six years I would see him often. He spoke to me as an equal, though I didn't pretend to be any such thing. After all he was a major and though I managed to make Specialist 5th Class, otherwise known as Spec-5 by the end of my service time, I had the greatest respect for my former teacher and now commanding officer.

When it came time for me to either re-enlist in the reserves or end my military service, Mr. Collischonn gently tried to convince me to stay. Yet by that time I had a daughter and a son and my own business. I decided to leave.

A few years later I moved away from my home state and lost track of Mr. Collischonn. My cousin Jack, also a teacher in the Wilton school system for many years, knew Mr. C and sent me a note announcing his retirement. A few years later I got a letter from a classmate who still lived in our hometown. In the letter was a copy of the obituary from the *Danbury News Times,* complete with the life story of Mr. Collischonn.

He was and continues to be a major influence on my life, that rare combination of a confident, powerful figure of authority combined with a gentle, often humorous manner serves as one of my greatest lessons and one of my fondest memories.

Mr. Z

Last December I got a Christmas card from my high school gym teacher, Nick Zeoli. He's 92 years old and living in Vermont with his wife Jody. "Merry Christmas, Tony. I'm doing great, walking a mile a day and I played over 100 rounds of golf in 2016." Somehow that did not surprise me. Mr. Z was a ball of fire from the first day I met him in my 7th grade gym class. "All right you meatballs, climb that rope." Yes, he called us all meatballs. Since a good portion of my classmates were Italian-Americans no one gave it a second thought. We were all too focused on the rope that hung from the gym ceiling, a big knot on the end of it. We all made it up the rope and back down again because behind that loud, booming voice was a man with a gentle nature, a solid support system that each of us could feel from the first time we met him.

Nicholas Zeoli was born in Saugatuck, Conn. on July 1, 1923. He grew up in what was known as "Little Italy." His family, like most in the neighborhood, had a large garden with lettuce, tomatoes, peppers, squash, potatoes and cabbage. Nick's father built a barn behind the house and put in a large oven for baking bread. Each Thursday morning neighbors brought their own dough and baked large round loaves of bread that would last a week.

The neighborhood was close-knit, and the adults kept an eye on all the kids, their own and others. Mr. Zeoli grew up in that neighborhood and graduated from Staples High School in 1942. His grades were good enough for college, but there was a war going on so he enlisted in the U. S. Navy, serving in combat in places like Saipan, Iwo Jima, Eniwetok and the Philippines.

After serving in World War II Nick earned his bachelor's degree from Arnold College (now part of the University of Bridgeport), then got a master's degree from Columbia University. He started his teaching career in Wilton in 1953.

In his 41 years of teaching and coaching he would touch the lives of more than 40,000 students. As football coach, his Wilton Warriors finished the 1961 season as undefeated state champions. His quarterback was a young man named John Corr for whom a courage award is named. You'll learn more about Johnny Corr elsewhere in this book.

Mr. Z gave his heart and soul to his Wilton students and his community of Westport through countless hours of volunteer work. He is most proud of his years with the Special Olympics. In 1991 he traveled to Pakistan to work with teachers of handicapped students on soccer and track and field skills. He did the same two years later in Bangladesh.

Following high school, I served in the Army and opened my own barber shop, I began a career in sports writing at the local newspaper and radio broadcasting at WMMM in Westport. Mr. Zeoli was a frequent guest on my show and during halftime of dozens of high school football games.

After retiring as head coach Zeoli became athletic director at Wilton High School and was the driving force in helping design and build a state of the art fieldhouse, later named the Nicholas Zeoli Field House.

I graduated in 1962 and have been the emcee for every one of our reunions since 1972. Nick Zeoli has been a featured guest at most of those reunions. He is and always will be a big reason for my positive outlook on life.

Mr. Zeoli is a perfect example of a giant of a man inside a 5-foot-6-inch, 150-pound body.

Mr. Mack

During my sophomore year at Wilton High School I decided to take art as an elective. I always enjoyed drawing and painting and frankly thought it would be an easy and fun course. The teacher was one of the most joyful, positive individuals I'd ever met. His name was Ed Mack. My sister had taken art with Mr. Mack three years earlier and really loved the class. Actually, I never met anyone who didn't like Ed Mack.

Not long into the school year Mr. Mack had us work on still-life sketching. I mean, how tough can drawing a peach and apple be? As it turned out, quite tough indeed. In fact, I had no talent for apple drawing and less patience, but I did my best. Thank goodness the following week we moved on to oil painting and were allowed to create anything we wanted. Now that's my kind of class.

I took four small squares of cardboard and four tubes of different color paint and made several straight lines, triangles and squares on my canvas. The finished piece resembled a poorly designed quilt and wouldn't stand a chance if put up against the work of some of Mr. Mack's better students.

As Mr. Mack toured the class commenting on each student's work, I wondered how in the world he'd have anything nice to say about my painting. I should have known better. As the gentle, kind, funny man breezed from desk to desk he stopped briefly at my canvas and said quietly with a wry smile on his face, "Tony, you certainly have a genius for design."

Make no mistake about it, I knew he was joking, as did my classmates. But I still loved the comment and I'll never forget it. He didn't go out of his way to set me up for a laugh; he went out of his way to say something nice about a painting that may have been my best effort but not very good.

I learned a lesson that day that has served me all my life. There is no need to make someone feel badly because of a lack of ability as long as they're really trying. Ed Mack saw that quality in all of his students and as a result that respect was returned.

While writing my first book, *Smile in the Mirror,* in 2002, I did some research and contacted Mr. Mack. He had retired from teaching in Wilton after 35 years and had moved to Mesa, Arizona. By no means was that the end of the story. In fact, it was just the beginning of a new chapter.

When he moved to Arizona he volunteered for the Heard Museum Guild, the Arizona Museum of Natural History, The Mesa Arts Center and two international organizations that sent him to Honduras and Guatemala as a design consultant to indigenous artisans and wood carvers.

He was recently honored with a plaque by the Arizona Natural Museum for his 20-plus years as a volunteer sculptor. One of his proudest achievements was the re-creation of a full-sized Pteranodon sternbergi, a bird-like dinosaur with a 24-foot wingspan.

I sent Mr. Mack a copy of my book, and we stayed in touch regularly after that, exchanging occasional letters and Christmas cards.

Then in the spring of 2016 Lyn Mack, Ed's daughter, phoned me to let me know that he was being treated for cancer and would most likely not live out the year.

Thank goodness my mother taught us all to approach life and death with the same attitude. Just because someone you know is dying, it doesn't mean they want contact or love any less than before. In actuality, they may need it more than ever.

I immediately called Mr. Mack, and we talked for several minutes. He joked about his failing health and talked of hanging in there as long as he could. We stayed in touch every couple of weeks.

In mid-August I was invited to speak in Sumner, Washington to a large group of teachers and school administrators. I arrived early, as I always do, and sat in the parking lot for several minutes thinking about my talk. I called my sister, also a retired teacher, in Connecticut, and brought her up-to-date on Mr. Mack's condition. At that point he had only weeks to live.

Just before going into the school to do my talk I decided to call Mr. Mack. "Hello, Mr. Mack. Sorry to bother you, but I'm speaking to 200 teachers in a few minutes. Do you have any suggestions?" He laughed and in a voice clearly weakened by cancer he said, "Tony, I know you. You'll say the right thing." We talked for a few minutes, then said goodbye. Mr. Mack died a few days later.

I am so grateful to have been able to visit with him on the phone, tell him I loved him and let him know how he helped shape my life so many years earlier.

The most important profession in the world is teaching. No one can succeed, in any field, no matter how much natural ability they have, without the help of teachers. I will always be grateful for the patient men and women who helped guide my life while doing the most important work there is, teaching.

A Reason to Smile

My daughter Lisa called the other day to say she's going back to school to get her teaching degree. Looks like she'll follow the example of my sister Mary Jane, who waited until her children were established in school and then started a career in teaching. Lisa will make a great teacher.

CHAPTER FIFTEEN

Mom

"God is right there before you."

– Mom

In every gathering of people there is a leader. In the military or in government it's fairly easy to identify the leaders, at least by title if not by their actions. In families identifying the true leader is much less obvious. Standard thinking when I was a child established the father as the leader of the family. As great a leader as my father was to all of us, my mother Mary might've even been better.

Behind the sometimes rough façade of my father's daily actions was the quiet, calming effect of my mother's love and guidance. I almost feel guilty that I was afforded the luxury of a mother and a father who, though not perfect, raised me with a combination of discipline and love that shaped my life.

Rutland, Vermont

Mary Louise Romano was born on September 15, 1912 in Rutland, Vermont to Nicholas and Filomena Romano. Grandma and Grandpa had emigrated from Italy in the early 1900s and settled in Rutland.

When my mother was in her late teens the family moved to Norwalk, Conn. where Grandpa Romano opened a grocery store. That's where Mom met a young barber named Tony Ventrella. They were married on September 20, 1932 in Norwalk. Shortly after that my grandparents moved back to Rutland, where they opened Romano's Bakery on Meadow Street and ran it for 40 years.

The Children

In December 1933 my brother Phillip was born. At the time Dad operated a barber shop on Main Street in Norwalk with his older brother Pete and a young employee named Paul. The same shop is still in business today, operated by a man who purchased the business from Paul when he retired 20 years ago. I stopped in during the summer of 2015 to say hello. Nothing has changed except the price of a haircut. Eighteen dollars now, up from 50 cents in the 1930s.

My mother had a baby daughter in September of 1939 and named her Joan. She lived only a few months before passing away in January of 1940. It was unclear if Joan died of pneumonia or had the early signs of cystic fibrosis.

My sister Mary Jane arrived in the summer of 1941, followed by me three years later and my sister Bunny a year after that.

Bunny was frail and sickly in her early years and never really had a comfortable day in her short life. She battled cystic fibrosis long before any of the advanced procedures of today were available and was in and out of the hospital her entire life.

Mom & Dad 1933

Seeking Solace

A couple of years after Bunny was born my Aunt Jane, who lived in New York and was close to my mom, suggested she try a new church that had helped her grow spiritually and become, she felt, a better mother and wife in her own family.

So one summer my mother attended a Christian Science lecture with Aunt Jane in Scarsdale, New York and a few weeks later joined the church. Mom studied and practiced Christian Science for the rest of her life and brought us up in the Sunday school and church.

Christian Science

There's a lot of confusion about Christian Science, and while I seldom talk religion to anyone I'll clear it up right here. Christian Science is the study of the life and healing powers of Jesus Christ. Most members of the church do not use medicine, drink alcohol or smoke, but there is no such rule on the books that makes that practice mandatory. It is a common sense religion that teaches love of the Bible and encourages study of the textbook *Science and Health with Key to the Scriptures,* by Mary Baker Eddy.

My mother and sister Bunny found great comfort in studying what we called "the books" during Bunny's frequent hospital stays. As a matter of fact, in her final days Bunny was lying in a hospital at Yale New Haven reading her *Science and Health* when one of her doctors asked, "What is that you're reading, Bunny?" She looked up, smiled and said, "That's *Science and Health*, and I've been reading it my whole life." The doctor patted her on the arm and said, "Well, Bunny, I like that idea. You keep reading it."

Several days later, after she passed away, that doctor told my parents that faith had indeed played a large role in her living as long as she did with cystic fibrosis. "Your daughter defied medical science by living as long as she did. She probably extended her life by three years just because of her faith."

Mixed Year

For a Yankees fan like me, 1956 was a great year. The Yankees won another World Series and a young star named Mickey Mantle won baseball's Triple Crown, hitting .353 with 52 home runs and 130 runs batted in.

Earlier that year, on March 12, my sister Bunny died. I remember getting off the school bus and walking to my house to find only my sister-in-law Fran at home. She had been crying. "Anthony, your sister Bunny died today," she told me with tears in her eyes. "Your father and Phil have gone to New Haven to settle things."

Bunny's Letters

My brother Phil was particularly crushed by Bunny's passing. During his two years in the Army in Germany it was Bunny who wrote him regularly, asking when he was coming home. Even today, so many years later, he becomes emotional when the discussion turns to Bunny.

A Short Walk

One moment in my life that will always stand out is the short walk with my mother in the cold drizzle of a March afternoon, from Bunny's gravesite at Riverside Cemetery to the car, following the burial service. Surrounded by relatives from both sides of the family, many showing outward emotions, my mother remained calm as she explained to me my sister's passing and how the sadness it brought would someday be replaced by gratitude.

At the time I took that little conversation in stride. After all, Mom always made sense with her explanations of life and death. Years later however, when I thought about it, I realized how extraordinary a woman she was to take one of the most devastating moments in her young life and turn it into a lesson for her other children and an example for the adults around her.

Lady Barber

My father opened a new barber shop on Route 7 in Norwalk in a building that had been a feed store in earlier years. I remember the shop well for a number of reasons. First, it had a special chair for kids that was actually a toy fire engine on a lift. Every young boy who hated getting a haircut would hate it a little less because of the fire engine. The Tootsie Roll candy they got afterwards didn't hurt either.

The other feature of Ventrella's Barber Shop was the lady barber who worked two chairs down from my dad. That lady was my mother, the first female member in the history of the Norwalk Barber's Union. Dad would recall years later the first union meeting my mother attended. The president of the union opened the meeting with, "Welcome, brothers and sister," as he glanced at my mom, standing in the back of the room.

My mother was a great barber, the favorite of many men who came into the shop. She also cut women's hair, which made her an important asset to the business. Mom and Dad worked side-by-side for years in that shop. She loved it, and he loved having her there. After all, now he could get away and go hunting with friends while leaving mom in charge of the shop.

My Advisor

I was fortunate to have a nearly perfect combination of parents in my youthful years. My dad was a little rough around the edges, yelled on occasion and made sure I had a good long list of after-school chores to keep me busy.

My mother, on the other hand, was much lower key, didn't raise her voice unless absolutely necessary, yet still got us to obey her most of the time.

Holiday Magic

No matter what crisis any of us were experiencing the holiday family gatherings usually took the edge off. I remember countless Thanksgiving Day dinners and Christmas Eve parties at our house and cannot think of one single disaster that ever occurred.

One of the reasons for this may have been that we didn't have any drinkers in the family. Alcohol was not only not the focal point of our holidays, it didn't exist at all. Thanksgiving and Christmas was about great homemade food, a lot of discussions about all topics and, most of all, laughter.

It was also a time when football on television was almost nonexistent. We actually enjoyed each other's company instead of turning our focus to a big flat-screen on the wall.

Don't get me wrong, I love football on Thanksgiving or any other day, but we didn't have it as a distraction when I was a kid, and I think it led to better family discussions than we're able to have today.

A Boxing Fan

I remember one night in the fall of 1962, sitting on my bed listening to the Sonny Liston versus Floyd Patterson heavyweight championship fight. My mother came into the room, heard the radio and asked, "Who's fighting?" I told her it was the title match with Liston a heavy favorite over the smaller Patterson. Instead of a courtesy nod, she sat down and asked if she could listen too. The fight only lasted one round, with Liston winning by knockout, but my mom and

Mom doing crochet

I sat there for a half-hour as she told me stories about her brother Jack who had been a professional boxer in the 1930s. Any mom that'll listen to a boxing match on the radio with her son is a special person.

As my mother aged she didn't slow down much. In fact, she started trying new things in her 60s and 70s. She began to do oil painting, even taking a class in it. I still have a few of her paintings now. She always crocheted, making blankets for all of her grandchildren practically until the day she died. I still have several beautiful wool blankets around the house and they're a wonderful reminder of my mother.

She always had an interest in opera and would often listen to it on the radio or record player. In her later years, as she sat alone reading or knitting, she would sing softly to herself with a peaceful smile on her face.

You Left Me Today

In October of 1998 my dad died while mowing the lawn in his Danbury backyard. Mom discovered him when she looked out the window. He died on his way to the hospital. My nephew Tony stayed with Mom immediately after the medic took my father away, and later that night Mary Jane drove in from upstate Connecticut.

I flew out of Seattle on a red-eye, arriving at 9 a.m. the next morning. When I got to the house my mom was sitting on her couch in the living room. I went over and hugged her, and asked her if I could read the Christian Science lesson to her. She read it every day and took great comfort from it. As I read for the next hour, Mom sat quietly with her hands folded and a peaceful look on her face.

Late that afternoon I went to the kitchen to get a snack and looked at the wall calendar I had sent my parents for Christmas. There in the little square on October 19 written in my mother's script were the words, "You left me today."

Florida Bound

The following month we had Thanksgiving at my niece Lorna's house in Old Saybrook. It was the first Thanksgiving without Dad and it was a difficult time for me personally.

He had always said the pre-Thanksgiving prayer, and now that honor was passed along to me. As hard as I tried to compose myself I couldn't get all the way through the prayer. The family understood and even laughed about it, but it was a major crossroad in the lives of us all.

After living in the Danbury house for a year, then trying an assisted living apartment in nearby New Milford, my mother moved to Florida.

There, for the next ten years my brother Phil and his wife Fran took care of Mom, saw her daily, attended to her every need and showed her the love that she had shown all of us for so many years.

Then, 20 minutes past midnight on December 26, 2009, Mary Ventrella, who had touched so many lives with her kindness, humor and love, quietly passed. She was 97 years old.

When I think of my mother I see her smile and hear her voice. "God is right there before you, dear." Whatever sadness I feel is always replaced with love and gratitude.

A Reason to Smile

Every Sunday in church I look to my left where my mother used to sit, and I think of her trying to unwrap a hard candy during the service. She didn't seem to notice what a loud sound it made. It still makes me laugh today.

CHAPTER SIXTEEN

The Lost Art

"The word that is heard perishes,
but the letter that is written remains."

Every two weeks for years after my father's passing, I received a handwritten letter from my mother. She had beautiful cursive handwriting, something that's not even required in many schools now. Mom always described the weather, something she read in the Bible and news about my Connecticut relatives. Every letter ended the same. "God is right there before you." Mom passed away on Christmas night in 2009. Sometimes when I miss her most I'll read one of her old letters, it provides great comfort no matter what's happening in my life.

The art of letter writing has gone the way of the typewriter, local bookstore, home telephone and decent meals on airlines. There's nothing I can do about most of that but I can still write letters and I always will.

Every Sunday night I write to my 92-year-old Aunt Jane in Ridgefield, Connecticut, my sister and her husband Earl in Connecticut and my brother and his wife Fran in Florida. Aunt Jane doesn't write back anymore since a recent fall has made it difficult for her. She does call occasionally with news of the family and the weather in New England, but I still write to her because I know how important it is to receive a letter that someone took the time to devote to only you.

My sister Mary Jane still writes about once a month and is brilliant at it. I've told her over and over she needs to write a book. Until she does I've included one of her letters in my book. It was a letter included with a card to our Aunt Helen

TO
Tommy + marland
and aunt
Jane and
uncle BoBBy

Dear Aunt Jane,

Thank-you for
the bradit and
books and flowers
and the things you
put on the table. you
know the little elfs.
I liked them very
much. my doctor
said I could take
the oxygen tent of
on monday, I hope I
will be able to breath
good with it off or else I'll have to
~~have~~ hane it back on again. he said I
looked much better and looked like I had
much more color in now. Well I hope to
be out very soon anyway.
Well Thanks- again for the gifts.

With lots of
love Bunny

Letter from Bunny

Demott on her 100th birthday. A few kind and thoughtful words written on a piece of paper for the sole purpose of making the recipient feel good.

There are hundreds of books written about letters home from war zones. From the Civil War to the actions in the Middle East, the letters strike the heart and soul of the reader. That's what letters are supposed to do, and that's why I think the lost art of letter writing is a crucial missing piece in modern society.

I remember writing to my parents and my sister when I was away at Army basic training and later on active duty hundreds of miles from home. I'll never forget the first "love" letter I received from a girl in Vermont over 50 years ago. We'd had only one date at the Rutland Fair and exchanged letters for a few months before the romance fizzled, but the impact of those letters has stayed with me my entire life.

Dear Tony,
I heard about the broadasting on wane TV. I think its really great! I hope I can make it to the Whiffle ball Marathon. I'm Looking Fourard to everything, Cant Wait! Although I dont watch Your Sports-easting. Just kidden! I do watch your sports-casting though! Thanks for everything I gotta go now. Sorry.

sorry so messy   See ya Saturday   Rick

Letter from Rick

I've included two letters in this chapter, one from Rick to me in 1981 and one from my sister Bunny to our Aunt Jane Ventrella in 1955. I hope these examples of handwritten emotions will inspire some of my readers to take the time to jot down a few thoughts, put them into an envelope and send them out to someone who might need a little boost.

I'm as impressed by modern technology as the next person. I think Twitter, Instagram and Snap Chat are fascinating and entertaining ways to communicate but I honestly don't think any degree of moving graphics, sound effects or animation can replace the raw emotion of a handwritten letter.

A Reason to Smile

I love to write letters and still do to friends and family around the country. That makes me smile just as much as receiving a letter from one of them.

CHAPTER SEVENTEEN

My Dad

"Let me show you where you're making your mistake."

Dad

Funny how 20 years seems like a tenth of a second when you look back at it. My dad passed away on October 19, 1998 while mowing the lawn. He loved to mow the lawn; it gave him a feeling of accomplishment, and it was good exercise.

He also loved fishing and taking his beagles into the woods to listen to them trail a rabbit. He loved the outdoors, his garden and his family. He loved being the center of attention on holidays, playing the spoons to entertain the little ones and, most of all, reading the Thanksgiving Day prayer with the family sitting around a large dining room table.

He wrote those prayers himself usually on a piece of white paper in pen or pencil. He always made sure to say something about everyone at the table, thanking them for coming from far and near to be with the family. He thanked my mother last, which always brought a smile to her face and tears to everyone else's. There was something powerful and yet reassuring when Dad mentioned how important my mom, his wife, was to him and the family.

After Thanksgiving dinner, we all sat around the table while Dad reached into the cupboard for a large empty fruitcake tin. He'd been given the actual fruitcake years earlier by one of his barber shop customers. No one liked fruitcake, and it sat uneaten for years before my mom tossed it out and kept the tin which had colorful Christmas illustrations on it. One year we all decided to write our names on a piece of paper and drop it into the box. I made sports predictions, my brother Phil tried to forecast the stock market, my sister mentioned some school news while aunts and uncles wrote about new babies or jobs or the recently hot summer that just passed. We wrote notes in that box for nearly 40 years. Obviously we needed more boxes after the first few years. It was a wonderful tradition that I will always remember.

My dad did not have a formal education. Actually, he left school in 8th grade and got a job to help the family survive. My grandfather worked in a hat shop in Norwalk, Conn., making a small wage, so the family chipped in any way they could. At age 16 Dad borrowed some money and opened a small barber shop. He would work in that business for the rest of his life.

When I turned 14 Dad took me aside and said, "I want you to learn to cut hair. I don't care if you ever use the skill, but I want you to know how to do it." For the next six months Dad brought various cousins and friends over to the house for haircuts. He explained it as a win-win situation. "You get a free haircut and my son learns how to cut hair." After the first few months those free haircuts finally started to look like a bargain for my dad's volunteer customers.

By the time I was a junior in high school I was a pretty good barber and actually worked in Ventrella's Barber Shop on Main Avenue in Norwalk on

Checking
Thanksgiving
Box

Saturdays. I was paid $25 for the day, plus tips. That may explain why I was able to buy my first car a few days after I got my driver's license, a used 1957 Plymouth.

After my dad retired from his own barber shop he worked part time for his granddaughter's husband in Len's Barber Shop in New Milford, Conn. That shop is going strong after 20 years in business. The rest of the time he spent on some small river or stream fly-fishing.

It's an understatement to say that my father wasn't keen on the idea of my leaving the haircutting business to go into broadcasting. "Why would you leave a nice trade, your own business, to work for someone else all hours of the day and night?" Dad asked me a few months after I closed my own shop to work in radio. Now that I think about it, that's a great question.

You Were Right

In 1984 I was in my second full year as sports director at KING-5 television. News director Don Dunkel called me into his office and offered me a three-year contract at $50,000 for the first year. It was by far the most I'd ever earned in a single year.

I remember calling my father that night to tell him about the contract. This was not a man driven by money, although he always worked hard in the barber shop and often took side jobs to take care of the family. "Dad, I just signed a new three-year contract at KING-5. I'm going to make fifty-thousand the first year," I told him. He responded immediately with, "That's good, but remember money isn't everything." Of course he was right, but at the time it was a milestone for me.

I traveled back to Connecticut the following week, arriving at my parents' house around 10 p.m. My mother had enough food out on the kitchen table to feed the 3rd Army, and for parents who were usually in bed by 9 p.m. Mom and Dad were bright-eyed and ready to talk.

Just as we sat down at the table, my dad reached across to shake my hand. The only other time I remember his doing that was when he picked me up at the Norwalk train station when I got home from the Army. Now in the kitchen at my parents' house at 10 p.m. on a Monday night my Dad was reaching out to shake my hand. "I just want to say you were right," he said. I was stunned. "Right about what?" I asked him. "You were hell-bent on getting into broadcasting even though I thought you were crazy. Now that you've done it, I just want to tell you how proud your mother and I are, and that you were right."

This figure of authority had for the first time in his life deferred to his youngest son.

All I could say was, "No, Dad. You were right. You raised me to respect others, work hard, save money and shave people with a straight razor. All of those skills will serve me for the rest of my life, with the possible exception of the shaving part." We both laughed, my mom broke out the spaghetti and meatballs, and we sat in the kitchen and talked until midnight.

I made it a point to visit my mom and dad twice a year for the next 13 years. I brought my three children–Lisa, Tim and Pete–on occasion, and in 1991 my girlfriend, soon to be wife, Mika.

My dad loved Mika. He had a nickname for everyone. He called her "Mickey."

The last real person-to-person visit I had with Dad was in July of 1998, when we drove from his house in Danbury about 150 miles north to Vermont to do some fly-fishing. As a kid following my dad on some hunting trips I recall how fast he walked and how difficult it was for me to keep up. On our last outing together Dad was in failing health and often had to stop and sit down as we made our way downstream to a couple of his favorite fishing spots. I remember looking back and seeing him sitting on a large rock as I continued to fish a spot in the river. It was at that moment that reality hit. I sensed it would be the last time we'd be able to share that experience.

As we drove home I loved listening to him boast about catching four trout that day while I caught none. Just as he did years earlier, Dad explained over and over where I had made my mistakes on the river. It used to bother me when I was younger, but his words were music to my ears that day. He couldn't keep up the pace I remembered from years before, but he could still give a lecture with as much conviction and passion as he'd always had.

A few months later, in early October, I flew back home to visit my parents again. Dad wasn't doing well on that visit. He was having an issue with his gums and his feet were swollen. During most of the visit Dad sat in a rocking chair with a light blanket over his lap. This man who was constantly on the move for 86 years was suddenly sitting in a chair trying to smile and joke while feeling awful.

Like so many fathers of that generation, my dad never complained, he just kept doing what he needed to do, moving forward, getting a job done, helping out in the kitchen, teasing the grandchildren. It was never about him, always about someone else.

As I left the house for my trip to Newark Airport and my flight home, I gently kissed my dad on his forehead and told him I loved him.

He passed away 12 days later.

What He Loved

We've all heard the quote, "He died doing what he loved." That's usually reserved for someone who quietly passes on while playing golf or fly-fishing or winning at poker. I'm not at all certain that mowing the lawn fits into that

Dad fly-fishing

category. That's what my dad was doing on the morning of October 19, 1998 in the backyard of my parents' house in Danbury.

"He said he didn't feel well earlier in the day," my mom explained later, "so he went out into the garden to pull some weeds. Later he decided to mow the lawn. I looked out the kitchen window and saw him lying on the grass behind the mower," she continued. "I called my neighbor Sue, a nurse, then went out to see your dad." The nurse called 911 and within minutes an emergency crew was on hand. It was already too late.

My dad really loved working in the yard, not as much as he loved fly-fishing or hunting or his family, but yardwork was not considered work for my dad or much of his generation.

All of my life we had a big garden in the backyard. Dad grew tomatoes, lettuce, squash, beans, even corn. I don't ever remember going to the grocery store with my mom to buy produce. We didn't need it; we grew it.

My brother who's eleven years older than me recalls many times when Dad would take baskets of produce to families who couldn't afford fresh food. "He was always giving people tomatoes, peppers, lettuce, anything from the garden," Phil told me.

Legacy

I am not so naïve as to think everyone had a wonderful father. I'm also not quick to condemn the dads who were less than perfect. In fact, I place myself in that category. For every dad in the history of the world, there's a different story. Some were thrust into the role before they were mature enough to handle it. Others had good intentions but fell victim to the pressures of the world and tried to respond with alcohol or drugs leading to mental issues and bad decisions.

Love Wins

No government program, local laws, attorney, counselor or teacher will ever really be able to substitute for the leadership and love of good parents.

It is not for us as humans to judge others, so I won't do that here. I can only say how grateful I am for my own father and my sons, who are also good fathers. I will always pray for fathers to do what is best for their families.

A Reason to Smile

I can almost hear my dad's voice giving me advice when I'm not sure what to do, and that makes me laugh. He was usually right.

CHAPTER EIGHTEEN

Uncle Ralph

"We shall never know all the good a simple smile can do."
– Mother Teresa

Uncle Ralph was my mother's youngest sibling, one of ten children born to Nicholas and Philomena Romano on May 17, 1921 in Rutland, Vermont.

In his 86 years of life Uncle Ralph would face more physical challenges than anyone should have to endure, yet he did it with a smile and a constant search for the humor in everything he faced. He beat the odds, turning one obstacle after another into avenues of success up to and even after his passing in 2007.

Ralph's physical challenges began early in life when he lost the sight in one eye. He was so young at the time that he was able to adjust to a bad situation, and people who didn't know him had no idea he could only see out of one eye.

Young Ralph lived with his family above Romano's Bakery on Rutland's Meadow Street. The youngest of four boys in the family followed in his older sibling's footsteps by quitting school in the 9th grade and also working in the bakery. By the time he was 14 Ralph had the skills of a master baker.

The Romano Bakery was nothing like many of the shops you see today. It was a true "scratch" bakery, where everything was made fresh daily. In the Italian neighborhoods of the 1920s fresh Italian bread was the most popular item on the menu. Families would send their youngsters to Romano's on Saturday morning and the kids had all they could do to keep from breaking off a piece of the often still warm loaf and stuffing it into their mouths before they arrived home. Years later, in the 1950s, I remember dipping the fresh bread into the bubbling pot of spaghetti sauce my mother had on the stove for dinner. To tell the truth, "sauce on bread" was my favorite long before spaghetti and meatballs, lasagna or even pizza.

On June 29, 1941, now 20-year-old Ralph Romano married his girlfriend Rita Garofano at the Christ the King Catholic Church in Rutland. The world was at war, though the United States had managed to avoid the inevitable at least until December 7th of that year, when Pearl Harbor changed everything.

On May 30, 1943 Ralph enlisted in the U.S. Army. It was wartime and all able men were needed to serve their country. Even though he was blind in one eye, Ralph was assigned to non-combat duty at Fort Devins, Massachusetts. Later he was shipped out to Camp Ellis in Illinois where he taught baking skills to Army cooks. "Soft duty," was not to be for Ralph, especially with World War II raging. He was assigned for rifle training for eventual deployment to Germany.

One day on the way back from the rifle range the jeep Ralph was riding in went out of control and rolled down a rocky embankment. Just as Ralph's head hit the ground a mortar shell went off accidentally nearby. The timing of the impact and the shell's explosion would cause him medical problems for the rest of his life.

At age 23, the young Army sergeant from Rutland, Vermont found himself in a New York City hospital partially blind and paralyzed. As luck would have it, world-renowned journalist and radio broadcaster Walter Winchell happened to be visiting soldiers that day and stopped by Ralph's bed. Winchell looked at Ralph, smiled and said, "You'll be okay, soldier. What do you want to do with your life when you get out of here?" Placing a rolled-up piece of paper to his lips as a makeshift microphone Ralph replied, "I'm going to be a newscaster like you, sir."

Winchell just nodded his head and walked away. He could see how badly Ralph was injured and didn't want to give him false hope. What Winchell didn't realize was Ralph didn't know the meaning of false hope.

For many years after his honorable discharge from the Army Ralph suffered seizures, sometimes as many as three a week as a result of the injuries. He was fighting an uphill battle.

Early in 1951 Ralph got his first break. The Veterans Administration offered him an opportunity to attend school on the G.I. Bill. He jumped at the chance and enrolled at the LeLand Powers School of Broadcasting in Boston. He took 600 hours of course study and never missed one session, graduating at the top of his class in two years.

Ralph Romano, blind in one eye and nearly killed in an Army jeep accident, would spend more than 30 years in the broadcasting industry. He started in sports, then hosted a news talk show at WBVM in Utica, New York.

Over a period of several months Ralph began to question the ethics of the local mayor and eventually got him ousted from office. During those contentious weeks on the air Ralph would feel the wrath of the crooked politician, once having garbage dumped on his front lawn and another time having his house fire-bombed. No one was injured in either case except perhaps for the mayor, who got what he deserved.

Dodgers Pitcher Johnny Podres interviewed by Uncle Ralph after World Series 1955

In the summer of my 14th birthday my family drove to upstate New York to visit my Uncle Ralph and Aunt Rita. Ralph knew how fascinated I was with radio broadcasting, so he invited me to sit in the studio during one of his shows. He told me to go to the UPI machine and tear off the baseball scores from the night before. As I sat in the studio opposite my uncle the "On Air" light blinked on and Ralph said, "Now here's my nephew Tony with the baseball scores." He pointed to me, and I reeled off those scores without even thinking about it. From that day forward I was hooked on broadcasting.

In the early 1980s when the first McDonald's restaurant opened in Ralph's hometown of Glens Falls, New York, owner Ray Kroc personally asked Ralph to host the opening ceremonies. Kroc was so impressed with Ralph's wit and emcee talent he gifted him with a lifetime McDonald's hamburger card. Ralph would have free burgers for life. Kroc actually went one step further, offering Ralph and his wife Rita a McDonald's franchise for the unheard-of price of $15,000. Ralph recalled years later, "I told Rita we'd be in on the ground floor of a very successful business if we invested the money. She looked up from a boiling pot of spaghetti and calmly said, 'We are not putting our hard-earned money into a hamburger stand.' We never did get rich, but I also never paid for a hamburger again," said a smiling Ralph.

Mom &
Uncle Ralph

In 1983 after an exciting and satisfying career in radio in upstate New York, Ralph and Rita moved to Florida. The way Ralph used to tell it, "We moved to Florida, but then if you live in upstate New York and you turn 65 you have to move to Florida, it's the law."

Ralph and Rita moved to Dunedin, Florida and bought a comfortable ranch-style home with a screened-in swimming pool in the backyard. It would not be unusual to see Ralph sitting shirtless at the dining room table having lunch after spending an hour in the pool. Rita quickly found a job while Ralph transitioned into retirement, doing what he'd always wanted to, stand-up comedy.

From his first month in Florida Ralph began a string of 20 years' worth of comedy shows across the region. His goal was not to make money but to entertain people who just needed to laugh. He made it a point to perform free comedy shows for all the organizations that had helped him over the years. Between 1983 and Ralph's passing in 2007 he performed more than 3,500 shows for groups like the Veterans Administration, Knights of Columbus, Catholic Services and the Red Cross. He was so grateful for the doctors, nurses, other professionals and volunteers who had taken care of him during his time of need, he just wanted to return the favor.

Failing Health

During his 24-year second career as a comedian Ralph would face several more physical challenges, including diabetes and leukemia. To see him perform or sit by the pool and listen to his constant stream of jokes and funny stories one would never know of those challenges.

Uncle Ralph's Picks

I made it a point to write to my Uncle Ralph often during those years and one day invited him to fly to Seattle to appear on television as a football expert. The fact that he knew little or nothing about football or the Seattle Seahawks was not a concern of mine. I was sure the KIRO-7 audience would enjoy my uncle as much as I did.

He visited my wife Mika and me for about a week, spending the days walking the streets of Seattle and saying hello to everyone he met. He was an instant hit in person and on television. My idea was to have Uncle Ralph on camera in a pre-taped segment once a week just before the Seahawks game that weekend.

Here now is Ralph's weekly script, word for word: "Hi everyone, I'm Uncle Ralph. I'll have my football pick in a minute, but first did you hear the one about (insert Ralph joke here)?" Then he would follow that by flipping a coin and saying, "This week's pick, Seahawks by a touchdown."

I had Ralph record 16 of those segments, one for every Seahawks game, and we played one a week for the entire season. For me it was a way to repay my favorite uncle for giving me that opportunity as a 14-year-old many years earlier in Glens Falls, New York.

Christmas Show

In late 2006 Ralph was fighting a losing battle with leukemia and diabetes, but he insisted on doing his comedy shows. In mid-December, he got a frantic phone call from a friend at the local Knights of Columbus Hall. "Ralph, I need a favor. We have a banquet in two days and my emcee had to go out of town. Can you fill in for us?" Even though he had an appointment for a chemo treatment on the day of the event Ralph accepted the invitation. It would turn out to be his final show and one of his most memorable.

About a week later I got a letter from Ralph explaining what a great time he'd had with the group of veterans, seniors and volunteers at the holiday show. After telling jokes for 45 minutes Ralph noticed a gentleman in the front row in a wheelchair with a prosthetic right leg. Ralph looked at the man and asked, "Sir, I couldn't help but notice you're not laughing." The man replied, pointing to his leg, "If you had one of these you wouldn't be laughing either." Ralph jumped down from the stage, took out his glass eye and handed it to the man. "I have one of these and I'm having a ball." Everyone in the audience laughed, including the man in the wheelchair. Ralph's final show would turn out to be his best.

One More Stand-Up

In the early months of 2007 it was clear that Uncle Ralph's health was failing. I'm so grateful that my mother, who had moved to Florida herself to be closer to my brother Phil and his wife Fran, had a chance to take her baby brother Ralph out for dinner that summer.

As it became apparent that Ralph was nearing the end he was unfazed. In fact, he had a meeting with his grandson and asked him to perform a comedy routine at his funeral. Highly unusual, but exactly what one would expect from Uncle Ralph.

Funny Funeral

Ralph passed away in the fall of 2007. I got a call from my brother Phil who attended the funeral. "Tony, it was the funniest thing I've ever seen," Phil told me. "Ralph's grandson told jokes for 25 minutes while standing in front of the open casket. It was almost as if Uncle Ralph was watching the show with the rest of us." I'm convinced he was.

A Reason to Smile

Every time I think of my Uncle Ralph I smile. Sometimes I text one of his old jokes to one of my children, and they usually text another one back. He made us laugh. He'll always make us smile.

CHAPTER NINETEEN

The Little Red Truck

"Sisters are angels who lift us to our feet when our wings have trouble remembering how to fly."

One December long ago we lived in a small rented house on Ohio Avenue in Norwalk, Conn. My older sister Mary Jane had her own room, but my younger sister Bunny had to share with me. It was no big deal since she was 10 and I was 11, and we got along great for a brother and sister.

Bunny was born with a lung disorder later diagnosed as cystic fibrosis. Her breathing was labored, but she was a trooper. She did well at school, joined the Brownies and later Girl Scouts and always had a smile on her face. Bunny and I got into a lot of mischief as little kids. When were 7 or 8 years old we broke into my older sister's makeup kit and splashed powder and perfume on each other, then threatened to run away from home when we got punished. We actually got about 100 yards from the house before the promise of ice cream lured me back to the fold against Bunny's better judgment. "It's a trick," she told me. "There's no ice cream, you're going to get punished."

She was right, there was no ice cream, and thankfully the only punishment amounted to cleaning up the mess we made and apologizing to my sister Mary Jane.

With Christmas approaching my sister and I spent a lot of time wondering what we'd get that year. I had seen a remote-control little red pickup truck at a local store and really wanted it. Keep in mind remote control in those days meant two D batteries in the bed of the truck and an on-off switch. Once the truck was on there was no controlling anything; it usually smashed into a nearby wall.

Bunny wanted a doll, a couple of board games and a Nancy Drew mystery book.

On Christmas Eve, after our traditional Italian-American dinner of spaghetti, meatballs and a side seafood dish, my dad reached into the freezer for special chocolate eclairs with vanilla ice cream in the middle. What a treat.

About 9 o'clock we decided to go to bed. I figured the time would pass faster if I was asleep. It's a good theory, but it didn't work out that way. We were both too excited to sleep.

Our beds were on opposite sides of the room so we had to talk in loud whispers, something that comes with lots of practice. After about a half-hour we fell asleep.

Portrait of Bunny
by Michael Reagan

Around 3 a.m. I heard my sister get up to go downstairs to the bathroom. No multiple bathrooms in those days; we all used the same one.

When she came back into the room she jumped on my bed and started shaking me. "You got it, you got it! The little red truck, I saw it in under the tree!" she said in a voice a couple of notches louder than a whisper.

So much for a surprise. My sister had spoiled it. Five hours before we'd be opening gifts I already knew what I was getting. My parents had decided to put a bow on it and leave it unwrapped. I guess they didn't consider that Bunny would spill the beans on her return trip from the bathroom.

"Sorry, I didn't mean to spoil the surprise," she said, "but it's so exciting." I couldn't get mad at her, nobody could. I just said, "It's okay, I'll act surprised in the morning."

A few hours later we heard my dad's traditional Christmas morning whistle. One short whistle was our signal to get out of bed, rush down the stairs and start opening gifts.

Me, Mary Jane
& Bunny

Bunny got her games and a doll, Mary Jane got some makeup, some books and a record album, and I got my little red truck with the D batteries not included. The batteries were in my stocking. My parents thought of everything.

The image of Bunny smiling and happy on that Christmas morning so long ago is one that will remain a sweet and lasting memory for the rest of my life. At the time I had no idea that it would be our last Christmas together. Bunny passed away the following March at Yale New Haven Hospital.

Christmas seems to come around faster as you get older. I swear we just put the tree out for recycling a few days ago and soon we'll be looking for another one. I can't do the artificial tree. Tried it for one Christmas a few years ago. Gave it away a few days after New Year's.

I look forward to Christmas carols every year, a little bit of snow, even the lights in my neighborhood that resemble the SeaTac Airport runway on some houses. Even though Christmas does seem to come around every few months now, it's still special to me because it gives me a chance to feel close to my sister again.

Every year on Christmas Eve, after everyone else has gone to bed I walk outside into the front yard. If it's a clear night I pick out the brightest star I can find and stare at it for a minute. It's my sister Bunny watching over me. I look at that star and smile. "Merry Christmas, Bunny. I miss you and thanks for letting me know about the little red truck." I know she's smiling back at me.

A Reason to Smile

This may sound silly but it's true. Every time I see a red pickup truck on the road I think of my sister Bunny.

CHAPTER TWENTY

The Best Medicine

"Life is better when you're laughing."

onight Show host Johnny Carson, who ruled late-night television from 1962 until 1992, had a knack for getting laughs without saying a word. One of his classic gestures was to look at his watch if the audience gave a tepid response to one of his monologue jokes. The joke may not have gotten a laugh, but the gesture always did.

I've been a fan of comedy and theater ever since watching the old CBS *Ed Sullivan Show* on Sunday nights as a kid. Sullivan, who was not a funny man, certainly appreciated people who were. He was one of the early "king makers" on network television. If you made it onto the Sullivan show and got laughs, your career took off.

Carson did his earliest stand-up on the Sullivan show. So did George Carlin, Alan King, Bill Cosby, Shelly Berman, Jackie Mason, Joan Rivers, and Myron Cohen.

Carson Stars

When Carson got his own show in 1962 he continued the tradition of giving young performers their first shot at success. Among Carson's most popular comedians were David Letterman, Joan Rivers, Jonathan Winters, Steve Martin, Robin Williams, Jim Carrey, Don Rickles, Ellen DeGeneres, Andy Kaufman, Eddie Murphy, Jay Leno, Jerry Seinfeld, Chevy Chase, and Chris Rock, just to name a few.

Funny Family

I grew up with comedy in my family. My Uncle Ralph was a professional comedian who had the same agent as Jay Leno early in Leno's career. In fact, when Leno became a late-night star on NBC he called Uncle Ralph and offered to have him as a guest on the show. At the time Ralph's failing health kept him from making the trip from Florida to Los Angeles.

Most of my 33 1/3 record albums as a teenager were soundtracks of comedians like Bob Newhart, Jonathan Winters and Vaughn Meader, who did a wonderful impression of President John F. Kennedy.

My family was filled with comedians. Only Uncle Ralph made a living at it, but so many others made a life with it.

Grandpa Romano

The earliest funny remarks I recall came from my maternal grandfather, Nick Romano. My mother's father was a serious businessman and owned a bakery in Rutland, Vermont, but around his grandchildren he was funny.

He once told me about his college education, though I was fairly sure he barely attended high school. "You know, Anthony," he would say in a blustery, loud voice with a big smile on his face, "I went to college at VSP." My mom would interrupt and say with, "Oh Pop, don't tease the kids about that."

Later she told me that VSP was Vermont State Prison. My grandfather did indeed spend some time there for driving a decoy truck from Canada back into the United States during prohibition. He only served a couple of days at VSP, but it sure made a good story.

Uncle Ralph

Ralph was my mother's youngest brother, one of ten in the Romano family. From the first time I met him as a young boy until the last time I saw him in his late 80s he was telling a joke. "I'm on a seafood diet; whenever I see food, I eat. The secret to a good marriage is simple. My wife and I go to dinner twice a week; I go Monday, she goes Thursday."

Uncle Louie

On my father's side there was Uncle Louie Lapolla, married to my dad's sister Anita. We called her Aunt Nettie. Uncle Louie ran a small engine repair business in New Canaan, Connecticut. There was never a time I met Uncle Louie when he wasn't smiling and whistling. Actually, I learned to whistle because of Uncle Louie. Whistling is almost comedy. You're not really making someone laugh, but you're probably making them smile, depending on the tune of course.

Dummy Ducks

The one thing I remember over everything else about our family dinners is laughter. We laughed about everything. One Thanksgiving my dad, brother Phil and I went duck hunting at the Norwalk Reservoir. We saw nothing for the first hour then suddenly Phil said, "Hey look on the water, there's three or four of them just sitting there." Dad stepped up and fired two shots, so did Phil. Nothing. The ducks just sat there. That's because they weren't ducks; they were decoys, really good decoys.

"Hey who's shooting, what the hell's the matter with you," came a voice from across the water. My dad shouted, "Sorry buddy, they looked real," then turned to us and said, "Let's get the hell out of here. This guy's really mad." I'll never forget running back to the car with my dad and brother and laughing at the same time.

When we got back to the house where Mom, my sister-in-law Fran and sister Mary Jane were making dinner, I had to be the first one to share the news that Phil and Dad shot some decoys. Later, in our Thanksgiving box, Fran wrote, "The boys went hunting, shot Dummy Ducks." From that point forward whenever someone says "Dummy Ducks," everyone in the family knows they're talking about Thanksgiving Day 1957.

Best Medicine

I will always turn to laughter before I turn to any other solution. I'm not talking about "put-down" laughter, or bathroom humor or sex humor, so often used today by people who can't be funny any other way. I'm talking about honest-to-goodness, well-thought-out laughter. It really is the best medicine and I take several doses of it every day.

A Reason to Smile

This one's easy. I smile every time I check out one of my favorite comedians on YouTube, or think of a funny family moment. As it happens, the other day I was in a sporting goods store and got caught smiling at the duck decoys. That was a tough one to explain to the employee who asked me if I needed his help.

CHAPTER TWENTY-ONE

My Library of Friends

"Whenever you read a good book, somewhere in the world a door opens to allow in more light."

–Vera Nazarian

Twenty-five of the greatest motivators of all time reside at my house. They all live in my favorite room, a few feet inside my front door. Two white window-paneled doors slide apart, revealing a stone fireplace across the room, set inside a dark green wall with photos of John F. Kennedy on either side of a Will Moses painting of children playing football on a high school field in a remote, southern Vermont town.

On the left of the room is a bank of windows, on the right a floor-to-ceiling wall of bookshelves filled top to bottom with my friends, the greatest motivational authors of all time.

Leo Buscaglia, author of *Love*, which sold 18 million copies, takes up an entire shelf. Just below Leo is Og Mandino, whose best-seller *Greatest Salesman in the World*, continues to inspire millions of people across the globe to be better in every aspect of life. Dr. Wayne Dyer occupies his own shelf with books like *The Power of Intention, Manifest Your Destiny* and *No More Holiday Blues*.

On these pages I want to share with you some of the authors who've helped shape my life. It's up to you to find these books in your local library or bookstore or online. Believe me, they're all available, and they will enrich your life as they've enriched mine.

Here's a look at what my friends have to offer you.

The Power of Intention by Dr. Wayne Dyer

I met Wayne Dyer in 2004 while doing an interview program on a Seattle television station. In his wonderful book he explains the importance of "connecting to the source," which in my view is God. He explains that our constant devotion to keeping the connection to that source open will have a positive result in our lives. My favorite quote from *The Power of Intention* is, "When you change the way you look at things, the things you look at change."

Love by Leo Buscaglia

The author taught a class called "Love" at USC in the 1970s. He approached the topic in the purest sense of the word. One of my favorite quotes from *Love* is this: "When you love another, you become his mirror and he becomes yours."

The Greatest Salesman in the World by Og Mandino

Mandino tells the wonderful story of a camel boy named Hafid who learns how complete selflessness is the only real key to rich and lasting success. This tale of effort, failure, greater effort, greater failure and finally success will inspire even the most cynical reader. It is one of my greatest treasures.

The Butterfly Effect by Andy Andrews

Andrews is a modern-day Mandino and Buscaglia. In *Butterfly* he shares two stories of individual efforts that have incredible results affecting billions of people worldwide, not only now but for years to come.

These three books are a good start, but there are many more. Here's a list of other "friends" who have filled my life with love and a sense that I can make a difference in not only my own outcomes but more importantly the future of others.

The Power of Positive Thinking by Norman Vincent Peale
Tuesdays with Morrie by Mitch Albom
Man's Search for Meaning by Viktor Frankl
Raising Positive Kids by Zig Ziglar

Make Gentle the Life of This World by Maxwell Taylor Kennedy
The Power of Positive Thinking in Business by Scott Ventrella
Silent Night by Stanley Weintraub
David and Goliath by Malcolm Gladwell
The Joy of the Gospel by Pope Francis
Science and Health by Mary Baker Eddy
The Life Changing Magic of Tidying Up by Marie Kondo
Win Forever by Pete Carroll
The One Thing by Gary Keller
Grit by Angela Duckworth

Independent Book Stores

In the last couple of years there's been a resurgence of brick-and-mortar bookstores. A store actually called Brick and Mortar Books is now open at Redmond Town Center in Redmond, Washington. Owner Dan Ullom and his father, John, along with the entire family, have done a wonderful job engaging the community and surrounding towns.

I just read a story in *Vermont Life* magazine about that small city's reaction to the closing of a store called Book King after 43 years in business. Rather than fret over the loss of a city landmark, residents came together in an effort to replace it. It seemed like a longshot at first since online book sales were still eating up a huge share of the book business. That didn't stop the folks in Rutland, Vermont. They got in touch with the owners of Phoenix Books in Burlington, which replaced a Borders store in that city and was a huge success. Thanks to teamwork by both parties at city hall, the chamber of commerce and the Downtown Rutland Partnership, the city had a new bookstore open within two years. Phoenix Books is now thriving in Burlington and Rutland and, as owner Mike DeSanto likes to say, "Bookstores are a bit of a sacred place."

That's how I feel about my little home library.

Add to this list some of your own favorites, and please share their content with as many people as you can.

We are a society separated by the technology designed to bring us together. We must never forget why we are here on earth. It is not to consume every material gift available without regard for the well-being of others. Rather, it is to take care of each other, love our fellow man, protect our children and all children and prepare them to do the same as the torch is passed to the next generation.

A Reason to Smile

I just read a new book called *Heartless* by Marissa Meyer. It makes me smile because young adult novels that blend science fiction, fairy-tales and romance are not usually my first choice, so this is a stretch for me. Besides, I got to meet Marissa at a book signing at Brick and Mortar Books recently. She's a terrific writer with a delightful personality.

CHAPTER TWENTY-TWO

Crossing Paths

"People who need people are the luckiest people in the world."
–Barbra Streisand

F unny how life is. You agree to show up at an event or a party even though you really don't feel like going and it almost never fails. You meet someone or learn something at the event that would've passed you by.

I've been fortunate enough in my life to have been in the right place at the right time over and over again. On the other hand, I've missed opportunities either out of fear of the unknown or a simple lack of interest. Here are examples of both.

Noel Johnson

In 1984 I ran the New York City Marathon. I had trained for six months and was thrilled to be among the 25,000 runners who shuffled across the Verrazano Narrows Bridge from Staten Island to Brooklyn on October 28th of that year.

I had mixed emotions about running the race since a two-year relationship with a young lady had ended days before and we still traveled together to New York. I almost didn't go. As it turned out, I'm glad I did.

We arrived in New York on a Thursday and walked over to pick up our numbers along with thousands of other people. Standing in line for two hours didn't seem so bad because I met so many other runners from all over the world.

There was a young couple from China running their first marathon together, a 22-year-old track and field athlete from Oregon State University, two nuns from Chicago joking about their running "habit," and a man from Norway I'll never forget.

His name was Noel Johnson. He was dressed in a track warm-up suit and New Balance running shoes. Some people notice hair, some fashion, but runners always notice what kind of shoes everyone else is wearing.

"I'm the oldest runner in the race," Noel offered, seeing that I was accompanied by a television cameraman and holding a microphone. "Really," I said, "how old are you?" That started a half-hour conversation with this fascinating man.

He stood 5-foot-6 inches tall, weighed no more than 135 pounds, had a full head of white hair, clear blues eyes and a deep tan. He looked like a marathon runner, and there was good reason for it.

"This will be my 25th marathon," Noel said, "and I'm 84 years old." That announcement was good enough to draw a small crowd around us. Noel went on to tell me his life story. At age 70 his insurance company cancelled his policy. He was a smoker, overweight and drank too much. "My doctor said I had two choices," he smiled. "Either change my ways or die." I chose to put off dying as long as I could," he said with a laugh. All the runners around us laughed as well. Noel was stealing the show on a New York sidewalk on a beautiful October afternoon.

At age 70 he gave up smoking and drinking and began to walk a few blocks a day. Within a month he was jogging, first a quarter-mile, then a half, full and soon two miles a day. "Once I ran in my first 5K (3.1 miles) I realized I was an athlete," he told me. "That's when I decided to step it up."

He went on to take his growing audience through his next two years of progress. Noel ran his first full marathon at age 72. It took five hours but he finished. He was hooked.

By the time he reached New York City in 1984 he was shooting for his 25th completed marathon.

Hot and Humid

I didn't see Noel on race day; too big of a crowd. As we headed off the Verrazano into Brooklyn I wasn't thinking of my 84-year-old Norwegian buddy, I was thinking about my 40-year-old self and how I was going to negotiate five boroughs of New York City on a very warm October day.

When we left Staten Island at 8 a.m. the weather was perfect. They call it "Indian Summer" back east, warmer than normal in late October but welcome since everyone knows that winter is right around the corner.

New York City
Marathon 1984

Warm October days are perfect for walking in Central Park or taking a carriage ride through the city, or even watching a World Series game at Yankee Stadium. But for running 26.2 miles, warmer than 75 is not a welcome thing. Through the third of the five boroughs it was 75 degrees and humid. I took water at every station, even walked a few steps so I could actually swallow since my body needed the fluid more than my chin did.

I have only sketchy memories of running through Manhattan since we hit the magic 20-mile mark there. At that point my running partner Sara, following off my left shoulder, noticed my foot fall getting lazy and said in a loud voice, "Do not stop running; don't walk, keep running." For some reason that made me mad and I picked up the pace just to spite her. It turned out to be the best move I made the whole day. I wouldn't have finished the race if she hadn't been there and said that.

I crossed the finish line in three hours, 47 minutes and 2 seconds, finishing in 3693rd place out of 25,000. Sara finished one minute later. We both wandered over to the recovery area and just laid on the grass, pouring water over our faces.

Lindy's

After a couple of hours we joined the rest of our group, all of whom finished and headed back to the Sheraton Hotel. I took a shower and headed back out for a walk. I was wiped out, had lost several pounds of water weight and was really hungry. I passed by Lindy's restaurant and recalled as a kid how great their cheesecake was. No excuses here, I'd just run 26 miles in 80-degree heat with high humidity. Some people would drink beer, I wanted cheesecake.

I walked in to find the place nearly empty, then I noticed a lone man sitting in a booth a few feet away. It was Noel Johnson. "Noel, how are you? Wow, what a hot day. You look great. How did you do?" He looked up slowly from his iced tea and said with a frown, "I didn't finish; the heat got to me. First marathon I didn't finish."

"Hey, no big deal," I said. "It was hot out there. Two-thousand people didn't finish, nothing to be upset about," I told him. Then he continued. "I ran fine for the first 20 but hit that wall hard with six miles to go. I walked in the rest of the way."

"You've gotta be kidding," I said, "you walked in? It was 80 degrees, you just ran 20 miles. Why didn't you take a cab?" "Noel Johnson doesn't finish a race in a cab," he said with a very determined look on his face.

We sat and talked for a while, and I could see he was beginning to cheer-up. "I don't feel so bad," he said. "I'll get number 25. In fact, I'm running a marathon in the spring." Before we said goodbye, Noel thanked me for the interview and the post-race pep talk then offered me a copy of his book. I picked it up at his hotel the next morning. It's title: *Noel Johnson, A Dud at 70, a Stud at 80*. I still have the book today.

Berlin Wall

Five years later my producer at KING-5 news, Dori Monson, now a very popular talk show host in Seattle, suggested we come up with some exciting national events to cover that year. I'd just signed a new contract that included travel to five sports events of my choice. Dori and I chose a World Series, Super Bowl, heavyweight title fight and the Kentucky Derby. That left one trip still to be decided. I made up my mind to run the Berlin Marathon that autumn.

I trained hard for months and got myself into terrific marathon condition, then I hurt my right ankle. Not only could I not train, I could hardly walk. I decided to cancel the trip to Germany. There would be no Berlin Marathon in my scrapbook.

My ankle healed well enough later in the summer to keep my running going. I ran a few races but put Berlin out of my mind.

That all changed on November 9th when the Berlin Wall came down. I would've been in Berlin with Dori and a television crew when the wall came down. I missed one of the great moments in history because I was afraid of a poor performance in a marathon. This is a blatant example of allowing fear to shut a door that may have led to a life-changing event. Dori still talks about it on his show.

Muhammad Ali

One afternoon I went to SeaTac Airport to cover the return of a triumphant local high school track team. As the team exited the plane I interviewed a couple of the kids and their coach. It would make for a fun feature that evening on the news.

In those days, the early 1990s, you could still meet an incoming flight at the gate. This particular flight was also a stopover from the East Coast on the way to Los Angeles. A few minutes after the track team exited, former heavyweight boxing champion Muhammad Ali stepped into the lobby, stretching his legs before the final flight south.

I seized the opportunity and did a short interview with Ali. He was gracious and kind to me. It is one of those moments when timing really was on my side.

Paul Newman

I'll be honest here. I've never been a big fan of auto racing, so an invitation to cover practice for a stock car race at Seattle International Raceway on a summer day was met with tepid response. "Be there by 12 noon because Paul Newman is going to test a car, and he'll talk to the media for ten minutes," the public relations person told me. "What the heck, I thought. Our viewers would probably love to hear from Paul Newman." So I drove to S.I.R. and got there at 11:50.

Right on the button at 12 noon Newman showed up. I'd seen a number of his movies and actually had a good friend who lived next door to Newman and his wife Joanne Woodward in Westport, Conn. I looked forward to doing the interview.

Two local newspaper reporters and a couple of radio producers began asking Newman a few questions about his racing experience and his reason for visiting Seattle. For some reason my photographer was late and my chances of getting an interview were growing slimmer by the minute.

Just as my watch hit 12:10 the KING-5 news car rolled up. "Sorry, we're done," said Newman's PR person. "He's going to drive a car now." Seeing my disappointment, Newman said, "Why don't you ride some with me?" as he stepped into the car. My photographer started to get in when Newman said, "Not you, him," pointing to me. "No cameras."

110 MPH

I scurried into the passenger's seat and quickly belted myself in, reaching over to shake Newman's hand. "Have you ever done this before?" he asked. "No, this is my first time," I replied. "Then hang on," he said, and off we went.

As we reached 100 miles an hour on the straightaway and began to head into a corner, I tried to make small talk with one of the most famous actors in the world. "My friend Bob Stillman was your neighbor in Westport," I said. "Yeah. I know the Stillmans," he replied with his eyes glued on the upcoming turn. "Hang on, this might get rough," he said.

Two thoughts came to mind as we headed into another turn at 95 miles an hour. First, what happens if we crash and we're both killed. The headline will around the world will simply say. "Beloved Actor Killed in Auto Crash." No mention of the poor sap next to him who didn't get an interview and whose friend lived next door in Westport.

"Oh, well," I thought, "he wouldn't be driving this thing if he didn't know what he was doing, and besides I've had a good life."

Oprah Winfrey

I worked at KCPQ in Seattle for a couple of years doing a morning news-talk show with Christine Chen. One day I had a chance to interview Oprah Winfrey.

Not exactly one-on-one but an interview nonetheless. I stood with six other reporters and cameras on a red carpet at a downtown Seattle hotel and did my interview with Oprah. "You're limited to two minutes, please," her handler told us. As she stepped in front of my camera I shook her hand and said, "You're a rebel. You did a show about people's good qualities and it was successful." She smiled and said, "Thank you, you're right. Television does not need to be negative." Her answer lasted about a minute. I thanked her and that was that.

Jimmy Carter

Former President Jimmy Carter came to Seattle for a book signing when he wrote *Hornet's Nest*. When I arrived at the University Book Store to do the interview, I was the only television reporter there. He walked over to me and introduced himself. "Do you want to interview me?" he asked with a smile. "Yes, Mr. President," I said. "I noticed you've been somewhat critical of the Bush presidency," I said. He laughed and said, "Somewhat critical? I've been very critical and here's why." I loved his candid and yet measured response. We had a great interview and he signed my book.

For all that's been said about Carter's presidency, I think I speak for millions of Americans who respect him for his devotion to people in need across the world. He is truly one of the great humanitarians of all time.

Danny DeVito

I worked at KIRO-7 television for 11 years, and one of the fun features I did as a sportscaster was called "Haircut of the Week." Since I actually worked as a barber for several years and had kept up my skills, I thought it would be fun to do a weekly feature during which I interview someone while cutting their hair. The actual haircut never really happened, but we did put each interview subject into a chair with a hair cloth over them as if they were getting a haircut.

One day actor Danny DeVito was in the building doing an interview on the radio when I intercepted him in the hallway with an offer to be on "Haircut of the Week." Little did I know at the time that DeVito had actually worked as a barber in New Jersey before being discovered.

The story goes that the producers of *One Flew Over the Cuckoo's Nest* discovered DeVito in his barber shop, asked him to read for the part and that launched his career.

So being the star of my little feature was not a stretch at all for DeVito. "Sure, I'll do it. Let's go," he said. "By the way, what's your name?" he asked. I said, "Tony." "Of course it's Tony. Hey Tony, give me a haircut," he said laughing. That's all we needed to do. I had my "Haircut of the Week," in one take.

I've been fortunate to have met thousands of people in my lifetime, many of them through the television business and my 11 years with the Seahawks. Some famous, most not-so-famous but all part of my life forever.

I look for the good in people. I've never been interested in how much money one makes, the kind of car they drive or their "status" in the community. They're all people, and that's good enough for me.

Joe Pepitone

In the early 1960s they were called "Bonus Babies." Young baseball players from the corn fields of Iowa to the sidewalks of Brooklyn. One of those rookies was a 21-year-old first baseman named Joe Pepitone.

"Pepi," as teammates called him, signed with the Yankees for $25,000 and made his Major League debut on April 10, 1962, my senior year in high school.

The Yankees were a team of aging stars by the early Sixties, winning the pennant and the World Series that year with Yogi Berra, Mickey Mantle, Roger Maris and Whitey Ford. Pepitone was going to be the next big star. The "toast of the town" in New York.

As it turned out the good-looking Italian kid from Jay High School in Brooklyn went from toast of the town to toast in a few short years. I'm not telling secrets here. Pepitone revealed his fall from grace in a book called, *Joe You Coulda Made Us Proud*, published in 1975, two years after he retired from baseball.

———•••———

Joe was going to be the next Mickey Mantle and Joe DiMaggio combined. He had a sweet left-handed swing that helped him launch 219 career home runs and 721 RBIs. He won three Gold Glove awards as a Yankee first baseman. That was all fine but nothing compared to what he could've been had he not spent much of his career in barrooms and bedrooms, trying to purge his guilt by drinking and chasing women.

Joe's father "Willie Pep" Pepitone was determined to make his son a baseball star. He was rough on the kid, beating him up often. Joe loved his father but one night after one of those beatings he yelled to his mother, "I wish he'd die." The next day Willie died and Joe blamed himself for years.

In those days fans never knew about players' personal lives. I didn't realize Mickey Mantle was an alcoholic until after he retired. Baseball writers forged friendships with players then and often protected them from reality. In many cases those same writers sat and drank with the players until all hours of the night and next morning.

So as a Yankee fan I had high hopes for Pepitone and so did everyone else in the New York area. Those high hopes were never realized. Pepitone did spend eight seasons with the Yankees though the team did poorly most of those years. He had short stints with the Cubs, Astros and Braves before playing one season in Japan with the Yakult Atoms.

Softball

In the summer of 1978 I was working at WANE TV in Fort Wayne, Indiana as a sportscaster. A local businessman had just bought a franchise in the American Professional Slo-Pitch League. Our local team was called the Fort Wayne Scouts and I was hired to do radio play-by-play. One day I got a call from the New Jersey team's public relations director asking if I'd be interested in doing an interview with a former Yankee player. "Sure who is it," I asked. "Do you remember a guy named Joe Pepitone?" came the reply. It turns out that Pepitone and a few other former major leaguers including Norm Cash of the Tigers were brought in to help boost fan interest. I agreed to interview Pepitone the next morning at the local Holiday Inn where the New Jersey Statesmen were staying.

I arrived in the hotel lobby at 11 a.m. as planned. The clerk rang Joe's room but there was no answer. As I started to leave the lobby and head back outside to my car I had to pass a long hallway with rooms on either side. Wandering towards me up the hall carrying a wine bottle in his left hand was "bonus baby" Joe Pepitone. He smiled and said, "Are you Tony, you wanna do an interview with me?" For the next 40 minutes Joe talked about his career, his reckless lifestyle and what might have been. Then he smiled, shook my hand and said, "Thanks for coming by, I'm glad you remembered me." "Joe" I said, "of course I remember you, you were always one of my favorites."

Later that night Pepi hit a long home run over the right field fence and I got to call the play on the radio. As I watched him round the bases in a slow-pitch softball game in Fort Wayne, Indiana in front of a crowd of 829 people I admit to feeling a little sad. The handsome dark haired Italian kid from Brooklyn with the perfect swing and gold glove was playing slow-pitch softball in Indiana. Sometimes life takes you in a direction you never expected and sometimes you take yourself there.

A Reason to Smile

You never know who you're going to meet today. Always keep a smile on your face and be ready to share it with someone. Who knows, that someone might just be a bonus baby, an 84-year-old marathon runner or a famous actor who likes to drive 90 miles an hour around corners.

Seven Keys to Happiness

1. Smile in the Mirror – Whenever you see a mirror, smile into it. You're a miracle. You're a living, breathing miracle. Are you flawed? Sure, but who isn't. Be grateful for a chance to live another day with an opportunity to make choices that will direct your life. You can choose to be happy or sad, and no one can control that without your permission.

2. Love Wins – "We all came here on different ships, but we're in the same boat now." That's Martin Luther King's wonderful quote from the 1960s. He was right then, and he's still right. It is up to each one of us to put away false pride and check our egos at the door. Cleanse yourself of all the negative chatter and embrace your fellow human beings. It's the only chance we have for a future.

3. Build Bridges, Not Walls – "Tear Down That Wall," is President Reagan's famous quote directed to the Soviet Union. In recent years a wall of a different kind has grown out of the dust, fueled by ego and stubbornness, fear and envy, ignorance and hatred. As human beings we have the power to reason together, live in peace together and make every phase of our lives better together. We also have the power to destroy each other and in the process destroy ourselves. I believe the choice is easy.

4. Make a List – At the close of each day make a list of everything that happened to you, good and bad, and express gratitude for it. Once a week make a list of the people who love and care so much about you. Get a mental picture of those people and keep it in your mind for when times get challenging. Once a month make a list of the successes you've enjoyed in your life. Remember

how each success made you feel. Once every three months make a list of all the things you take for granted, like clean water, shelter, your sight, sense of taste and smell, sound and feel. You're a miracle. There's only one of you in the world. Be proud of that.

5. Discard Bad Thoughts – In the few minutes between getting into bed and falling asleep try this exercise. Get a small pad or notebook and write down anything that's bothering you, including physical pain, mental strain, work problems, family issues, your "to do" list the next morning, anything you can think of. Now quickly flip the paper over to its blank side and put it on the night stand next to the bed. Close your eyes and mentally send that list of problems into space and out of your sight. Imagine an explosion that destroys all of those worries in a split-second. Now replace those bad thoughts with a pleasant memory and focus on it until you fall asleep.

6. Get Rid of Stuff – Why do you suppose *The Life-Changing Magic of Tidying Up* was such a success? Simple. We have too much stuff. My mother used to look at my room and say, "Cluttered room, cluttered thoughts." She was way ahead of her time. You'll be amazed at how liberated you'll feel when you purge the things you don't use anymore from your house, apartment and car. It really works.

7. Younger Next Year – Another bestseller I recommend is *Younger Next Year*, by Chris Crowley. It's all basic things we already know. It covers common sense ideas such as eating smaller portions of better food, exercising daily and staying away from the obvious killers like smoking, overuse of pharmaceuticals, alcohol or anything else that'll shorten your life. Nobody lives forever, but there are choices we can make to at least live better, healthier lives, not just for us but for the people who count on us.

CHAPTER TWENTY-FOUR

Here's Smiling at You

I understand there are a number of reasons people feel sad, fearful, and resentful, even hateful at times, but I will never stop waving the flag for love, understanding, curiosity, compassion and good old-fashioned positive thinking.

Some argue that these qualities must come from our leaders first. Don't hold your breath waiting for that to kick into gear. It's a nice idea, and it does help, but we cannot count on it, especially in the polarized political climate of recent years.

Oh, it's easy to long for the days of Ronald Reagan, John F. Kennedy and Franklin Roosevelt, all of whom spoke with passion and sincerity.

I'll never forget January 28, 1986, when the Space Shuttle Challenger exploded, taking with it the lives of all seven astronauts. In the president's address that evening he spoke directly to the youth of America, many of whom had watched the shuttle explode on live television. "It's all part of taking a chance and expanding man's horizons," Reagan said. "The future doesn't belong to the faint of heart, it belongs to the brave. The Challenger crew was pulling us into the future, and we'll continue to follow them." Reagan closed his speech with these words: "We will never forget them, nor the last time we saw them this morning as they prepared for their journey and waved goodbye and slipped the surly bonds of earth to touch the face of God."

Ronald Reagan mirrored the anguish of the American people that night, but he also reminded us that hope will never die and even through tragedy we need to keep moving forward.

Twenty-seven years earlier, on the steps of the U.S. Capitol, President John F. Kennedy told the nation, "Ask not what your country can do for you; ask what you can do for your country."

On December 8, 1941, after the bombing of Pearl Harbor, Roosevelt rallied a shaken nation with the notion, "We have nothing to fear but fear itself."

What Reagan, Kennedy and Roosevelt did on those occasions resonated with Americans in their time of need and doubt. We had our problems in each of those eras, but I think we at least agreed that solving them was everyone's responsibility.

My hope is that our leaders can find it in their hearts to shed partisan politics and do the job they were elected to do, and yet that's only part of the solution.

The rest is up to us. We love to blame politicians for everything and yet fewer than half the eligible voters in America even bother to register, and half of those who do register often talk a good game but don't vote either.

Whenever I'm tempted to blame someone else for my own failure I do a simple exercise. First, I point the index finger of my left hand outward and then I point it at myself.

The best way to change something in your life is to take responsibility, identify what needs to be done and do it. If you wait for the President, the governor or the mayor, you may be waiting a long time.

Finally, I don't want to hear the excuse that you're too old to make a difference. Youth is not a time of life, it is a state of mind.

Whether you're 19 or 90, there is in every human being's heart the lure of wonder, the unfailing childlike appetite of what's next and the joy of the game of living. In the center of your heart and my heart there is a wireless station: so long as it receives messages of beauty, hope, cheer, courage and power from men and God, so long are you young.